TRAVELS WITH DENISE
THAT WASN'T MEANT TO HAPPEN!

SHARON HAYHURST

Copyright © 2022 Sharon Hayhurst
Cover design by Joe Shepherd www.heyjoeillustration.com Copyright © 2022 Sharon Hayhurst

Production and formatting by AntPress.org

First Edition
The author asserts the moral right under the Copyright, Designs and Patents Act 1988 to be identified as the author of this work. All rights reserved. No part of this publication may be reproduced, stored in a retrieval system, or transmitted, in any form or by any means without the prior written consent of the author, nor be otherwise circulated in any form of binding or cover other than that in which it's published and without a similar condition being imposed on the subsequent purchaser.

Some names, places and other details have been changed to protect the privacy of individuals mentioned in the book.

This book is dedicated in loving memory of my mum, Jill Megaw.

Mum was the first person to read this book before publication, from her hospital bed. She was proud of my writing and got so much pleasure out of it. In fact I came in to visit her one morning and found a copy of my first book leaning on her bedside cabinet with a big handwritten sign next to it, directing staff to Amazon for online purchase. You were my number one fan, Mum, and I will always be yours.

In 2014 my darling cousin Pauline in Belfast, whom I've written about in the chapter 'The Red Witches of Belfast', passed away unexpectedly at the age of 53. She is survived by her beautiful daughter, Christine.

CONTENTS

The Beginning—Crabs	1
1979	
Fiji	
Golden Kiwi	9
1982	
New Zealand	
Beings, Baptists, Boys and a BBQ	19
1986	
Manchester, Northern Ireland and London	
Spooky Salford Slum	31
The Red Witches of Belfast	39
Send in the Clowns	47
1988	
Australia	
Heat, Huntsman and Horses	55
1990	
Canada	
Customs and Cooking	65
1996	
USA	
Thomas Tours the States	75
2004	
West Coast, New Zealand	
It Was Him. He Did It!	89
2006	
France and Italy	
The Catapult	97
Excuse Me, Sir. There's an Olive on Your Head	105
Spies and Stingers	113

2012
France and Italy

Cathar Castle Spectre	123
We've Been Watching You	131
The Gypsy Curse Begins	139
Grotto, Guns and Gypsies	149

2014
Italy

When Bicycles Go Bad	159

2016
New Zealand

Sammy the Salmon's South Island Sojourn	171
Kaikōura Quake Served with Kahlua	181

2018
Montenegro and Croatia

Captain Jack's Balls	191
The Smoking Germans	201
The Black Cat	207

2019
New Caledonia and Thailand

Nana's Suitcase	219
Honee, You Wan' Gel Nails?	229

2020
New Zealand

Fecker the Falcon's Wild Ride	241
COVID Toes and COVID Woes	253
Message from the Author	265
Author Profile	267
Acknowledgements	269

THE BEGINNING—CRABS

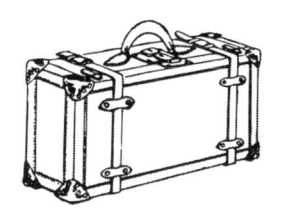

The school bus driver slammed on the brakes, stopped the bus and stomped down the aisle. His big boots narrowly missed crushing one of my crabs. He stopped at the offending bucket by my feet, noticing I was sitting perfectly still, red-faced, eyes lowered.

'Whose is this?' he yelled, making me jump as he nudged my bucket with his giant boot.

'Umm, mine, sir,' I squeaked, tentatively raising my hand, a bead of sweat forming on my top lip.

'This is not a zoo; look at this mess,' he growled, a deep frown forming on his weathered face.

Glancing down, I took in the puddles, sand, seaweed, shells and, oh yeah, crabs, lots of crabs.

'Get off my bus,' he bellowed. 'I'll be talking to the school about this.'

I gulped. 'That wasn't meant to happen,' I whispered, gathering up my bag.

My sister, Helen, looked away, taking the stance of, 'Who are you?' She left me to take my walk of shame down the bus aisle alone, snatching up my bucket on the way. *I'll never live this down*, I thought sulkily, hanging my head in shame. Thankfully I wasn't too far from my stop.

As I walked down my street, dragging my feet on the dusty pavement, I saw Helen standing at the letterbox with Mum; no doubt she'd filled her in about my crab situation. Mum had her hands on her hips. *I'm probably going to get the wooden spoon*, I thought.

I replayed the day's events in my head, slowing my walk while I formed an explanation for Mum. The day had started pleasantly enough, with a school trip to the rocky shore with the other five-year-olds. Buckets in hand, we'd eagerly explored the rock pools in the sunshine, collecting crabs and aquatic treasures. The other children had sensibly returned their live specimens to the pools before departing on the bus. But for some weird reason, I thought it would be a great idea to take my bucket full of crabs home with me. Goodness knows what I imagined I was going to do with them. Back at school I'd boarded the usual bus to go home and popped my bucket of lively crabs under my seat.

I would have got away with my crab smuggling if the bus hadn't lurched around a corner, knocking my bucket flying. I'd watched in horror as my precious cast of crabs spread across the bus floor in a tide of agitated clacking claws. The gang of cranky crustaceans located the enemy and homed in. What they found were toes, lots of them. It was summer and the children were wearing open sandals. I froze, mortified, knowing what was coming but too afraid to react.

An ear-splitting cacophony rent through the air as sixty frightened children leapt on seats, scrabbling for safety. Amid the caterwauling, one word could be heard clearly—CRABS! That was when the driver stopped the bus. It was game over for Denise. And that wooden spoon was heading for my butt.

Writing my first memoir, *Travels with Geoffrey*, had raised questions, with readers repeatedly asking, 'How could you be so unlucky? Why do so many unfortunate things happen to you?' This had got me thinking. Where did it all begin? Had I always attracted trouble, even prior to the arrival of my husband, Geoffrey? So I'd gone to the fount of all knowledge with this question—my mother. Mum's wee beach house, nestled next to the Waikanae River, was only about a twenty-minute drive from us on the Kapiti Coast. Visiting her one afternoon, I'd asked, 'Mum, when I was little, did I cause any trouble?' *Surely not, I was thinking.*

'You even need to ask?' She laughed, looking incredulous. 'How long have you got?'

I was already regretting my question, but it was too late.

'Well, what five-year-old do you know that has to be captured by a policeman on their first day of school? Little sod, you refused to get out of the car. Every door I dashed to, you scampered to the other side or climbed into the front or back to evade capture. I've never been so embarrassed in all my life, having to hail an officer of the law to help apprehend a five-year-old. Even then you didn't make it easy. It was like cornering a slippery hog. Everyone was staring and laughing,' she added.

'Well, that was your fault. I didn't want anyone seeing me after you cut around my hair with that pudding bowl and dressed me in that horrid, scratchy, green cardigan,' I pointed out.

Ignoring me, Mum carried on. 'And you were only at school for a few days before you made yourself sick, eating green Palmolive soap as some sort of new entrants' initiation. Shall we talk about that time you got yourself trapped in the neighbours' wardrobe and nearly suffocated to death? I mean, who does that?'

I sighed heavily. *Ask a silly question and now look what I've started.*

'Then there was the time you stuck that blue crayon up your nose while we were camping,' she began.

Oh, I'd forgotten about that.

'It got wedged so tightly up your nostril that not even the first aid staff could get it out, so they put you in the sun while we waited for the crayon to melt. You sat there with blue wax slowly dribbling out of your nostril, looking like a Smurf.' She laughed.

'Oh well, that's not so bad,' I said, ready to dismiss that conversation quickly, but Mum was just warming up.

'You were always causing trouble and don't get me started on dinner time. It was impossible to sit down together for a quiet family meal; you always turned it into a flaming circus, acting the clown and pulling ridiculous faces. Your father said it was like living with a court jester. But the silliest thing you ever did was taking those crabs for a ride on the bus. What were you thinking? That wooden spoon spent more time on your butt than in the pot.'

'You didn't even get me; you just used to chase me around the dining room table with it then give up.' I laughed. 'I think we'll leave it there,' I replied, hopping up and grabbing my car keys. As I left, Mum had followed me out to the car, gabbling on about the time I had to be rescued from a very tall pine tree. I sighed. Why did I even ask?

Now, driving towards home, following the river valley into the foothills of the Tararua Mountains, I chuckled out loud over the crab incident. As I glanced in the rear-view mirror, the 50-something face that stared back at me was thankfully no longer framed with pudding-bowl hair. While the familiar New Zealand landscape of bushy tree ferns, green paddocks, and sheep flashed by, my mind flicked back over some of my silly incidents, all of which have contributed to my reputation for attracting trouble. And there was I, thinking Geoffrey was to blame. Perhaps it had been me all along. Thinking back, I could pinpoint exactly where things started to go pear-shaped; it was the crab smuggling.

And so had begun the misadventures of Denise, some of which I'm about to share with you now. I'm sure most of them weren't my fault, possibly just some weird alignment of the stars when I was born. Someone up above thought, 'Here's a funny one; let's have a bit of a laugh with her.'

A little explainer before we move on. While travelling with our two children, they assigned us each a nickname after eavesdropping on some American tourists. The American names have stuck. So we have me (Denise), my husband, Geoffrey, and our two children, Jan and Don, whom you'll be introduced to in upcoming chapters. And then there are my parents who, once I had children, were known to all as Nana and Poppa.

On with the story.

1979

FIJI

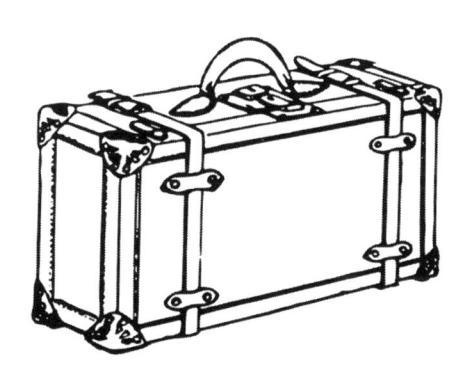

GOLDEN KIWI

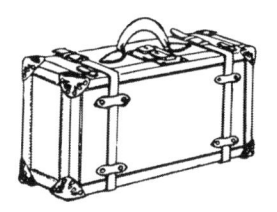

*I*t's winter 1979 in Christchurch, New Zealand. A housemaid called Jill and her workmates are gathered around the radio in the cleaning cupboard at the Travelodge hotel. They keep a furtive lookout for the boss. The five winners of the $100,000 Golden Kiwi lottery are about to be called out by name. Jill turns the radio up and leans closer as the announcer begins reading the names. Jill hears him call out, 'Ginger Beer Syndicate.' Time momentarily stands still. She gasps then lets out a piercing shriek, causing the other housemaids to jump.

'We've won; we've won,' she shouts, dancing around and hugging the other ladies. Jill is quickly dragged off to the office so that she can ring her husband at work. All thoughts of being furtive have flown out of the window.

Jim is at his desk on the 5th floor of an office block in Christchurch. He's in charge of a team of engineers at a computer company. An Irishman who likes a drink, he's a popular boss. He and three workmates have only recently formed the Ginger Beer Syndicate, named because of Jim's many failed attempts to brew ginger beer successfully in a cupboard at home. He answers the phone. His wife,

Jill, is on the other end, along with a posse of excited housemaids in the background.

'I think we've won the Golden Kiwi,' shouts Jill. 'I heard them call out Ginger Beer Syndicate.'

The phone goes dead. Jim is running around the office yelling. Phone calls are made and it's confirmed: the four of them have won $100,000, a share of $25,000 each. He calls his wife back, the emotion evident in his voice. It's true; they really have won the Golden Kiwi. Forget work. Jill rushes home to tell her girls, Denise, twelve, and Helen, fourteen.

Jim's the boss. Work is over for the day. The entire office heads to the nearest pub but none of them has enough money to shout the drinks. They tell the barman they've won the lottery and he agrees to give them a tab. Celebrations are underway.

When I was twelve years old, something very exciting happened. I was in my last year at primary school in Christchurch. My sister, Helen, and I got home from school this particular day and were surprised to see Mum back from work already. She looked pretty happy so it couldn't have been anything bad. She blurted out the news. We were now $25,000 richer. In 1979 this was life-changing. Helen and I stood staring at her, wide-eyed, mouths agape, as the news sank in. Breaking into wide grins, we hopped up and down, laughing with joy before listing our huge and selfish demands. We set the bar high. We wanted to have a roast chicken for dinner and a new pair of jeans each that weren't on sale. In hindsight we really should have aimed higher. But hey, we were living on mince, corned beef, and fish pie in those days. A roast chicken would be sumptuous and, up until then, it was something that was reserved only for Christmas Day.

The Golden Kiwi ultimately changed the direction of our lives, for without that money, my parents would never have bought a bach at

Motunau Beach. This little holiday home in a small beachside community in North Canterbury would eventually lead to major changes in our future and become our family home. Helen would meet and marry a local fisherman. Mum and Dad would end up buying the local general store and post office. And as for me, I would choose a different path. But all this was ahead of us and all brought about by winning the Golden Kiwi in 1979.

But now, Mum had money to spend. We were going on our first-ever family holiday overseas, something we could never have dreamt of doing before. She took a month off work from her cleaning job at the Travelodge, booked Lena, the poodle, into the kennels and packed our bags. We were going to the Pacific Island of Fiji.

So it was that in September 1979 we flew to Fiji for ten nights' holiday. After a sleepless night not far from the airport in Nadi, tossing and turning in the humid tropical heat, we presented ourselves at reception to wait for our ride. A beat-up, old taxi duly arrived to drive us the three hours on unsealed roads to Man Friday Resort on Fiji's Coral Coast. The resort was in the middle of absolutely nowhere, which is about where the taxi got a flat tyre. We bailed out while the driver changed it. Sweat drenched our clothes in the high humidity. Mum's '70s bouffant wilted, along with Dad's impressive moustache, as they both puffed on cigarettes. Underway once more, the car bumped down a long, dusty dirt road bordered by tropical vegetation on both sides. Helen and I stared out of the grimy taxi windows with interest.

Eventually we reached the coast and a warm Fijian welcome at the Man Friday Resort. Our accommodation was two bure-style, thatched-roof rooms on top of the hill. Our bures overlooked the grounds, pool and out towards the Coral Coast. Overhead, fans whirred around lazily in the heat. Everything felt new and exotic: swaying coconut palms, scented frangipani flowers and turquoise waters surrounded by a reef. It was heavenly.

Helen and I spent our time swimming in the footprint-shaped pool, playing coconut bowls, swinging in a hammock or slurping on watermelon. We sashayed about in our peasant blouses and long, tiered, gathered skirts popular in the '70s. Children from the neighbouring village met us on the beach most days and offered us bareback horse rides. Staff took us out in their boat to explore the marine life within the reef.

Every night we dined on fresh, fried reef fish then the village band would entertain us while the smiling Fijian staff taught us to do the Fijian shuffle. Some nights there was toad racing or hermit-crab races. On other evenings the adults played silly games like pass the balloon down the line of people without using your hands—tipsy adults, pressing their bodies together; talk about gross. Helen and I drew the line and swiftly exited; we were way too cool for that. Heading out into the darkness, we trod carefully to avoid the croaking toads that were all over the ground. We rode the little cable car up to our bure, hoping the Fijian golden orb web spiders were asleep. The nights were warm and the crickets chirped loudly. Flicking the light on when reaching our bure sent startled, little green geckos scuttling.

The guests at the resort had all been invited to attend a traditional Fijian kava ceremony in the neighbouring village so we caught the local village bus to Sigatoka to shop for suitable outfits for the occasion. We purchased an assortment of bright, tropical-print dresses. I chose a blue print to complement my dark-blonde hair and Helen chose a red and white one to go with her dark-brown locks. The dresses were light and cool to wear in the heat—a strapless bodice gathered at the waist with a full skirt.

The night of the visit arrived. Kava, the traditional national drink of Fiji, is commonly served as part of welcoming guests into a village. One of the men who worked at the resort and lived in the village led us all along the dirt track, explaining to us as we walked what the process was. When presented with the kava, we were told to clap once and shout *'bula'* (Fijian for hello) then drink the kava in one gulp if possible, clap three more times and end with the word *'maca'* (pronounced ma-tha).

He warned us that kava, made from the crushed root of the yaqona, is mildly narcotic and could create a numb feeling around our mouths, lips or tongues. 'Don't worry,' he assured us, 'a bit of kava and you'll be feeling calm and relaxed.' Calm and relaxed are not how I would describe what followed. In fact, it was the exact opposite.

As we approached the village, we entered a scene of small tin shacks and wooden huts on stilts. Chickens, pigs and dogs roamed about, scratching in the dust. Children we'd met during the week called out *'bula'* to Helen and me as we arrived. A man wearing a traditional Sulu skirt was waiting outside the meeting house and blew on a large conch shell. We filed in quietly and seated ourselves in a circle, ready for the ceremony to begin. I remember feeling scared in case I did something wrong.

The village elders were already seated and after welcoming us, they prepared the kava for drinking. Their chief was the first to partake then the kava was ladled out one coconut bowl at a time around the circle to each guest. By the time it reached me, I knew what to do: clap once, say *'bula'* then down the stuff. Easier said than done. It tasted like bitter, peppery, muddy water. But down it went before I clapped three times and said *'maca'*.

What our host hadn't told us was that after a few rounds of kava, the guitars would come out and the local village males, who had perhaps indulged in rather a lot more kava than the guests, could get quite frisky. A young man hopped to his feet and started prancing around on the woven mat as if he was being stung by fire ants, while waving his arms madly. The unworldly and inexperienced girl in me was horrified.

Oh boy, this is embarrassing. I didn't know where to look so looked at Helen. A grin spread across her face. Suddenly two big, strong, brown hands seized mine and hauled me to my feet. *Oh no, no, no, you've got to be kidding me.* I hadn't consumed enough kava even to remotely entertain the idea of strutting my stuff in the centre of a circle of strangers.

As a gangly, pre-pubescent girl on the cusp of teenagehood, this was just too awful for me. But what could I do? I couldn't insult the villagers. I mistakenly believed I needed to copy the young man's moves. And so I began to prance about like a dying daddy longlegs that had been zapped with fly spray. In short, I looked like a complete twit. My new, blue Fijian dress twirled as this lithe young man grabbed me and spun me around. I caught sight of Helen's face; she looked horrified. My cheeks blazed red and I wished the dance would come to an end. I tried to inch my way subtly back towards my empty place on the mat. But every time I thought escape was mercifully near, he would grab me again and give me an almighty twirl. My dress billowed high and my cheeks glowed. I silently willed it to be over.

Thankfully the torment finally drew to a close. The young man looked on the verge of collapse; he needed a top-up of kava. At last he released me so that I could slink back to my spot on the floor.

'What were you doing?' blurted Helen, looking at me like I was insane.

I shrugged. *Oh Lordy, how mortifying. Why me? Why Denise?*

According to my mother, my blonde hair had attracted him, blonde hair being a novelty in the islands. I can only wonder at that young man's choice of dance partner. I might have been blonde but I was sporting the worst-looking mullet haircut I've ever seen. The kava must have been good enough to affect his eyesight.

Before flying home we spent two nights in the capital city, Suva, where we purchased some eclectic souvenirs at the market: delightful shell bracelets and necklaces, a bamboo tray with matching coasters, plastic leis in a range of gaudy colours to match our tropical outfits, a teapot (weird) and the strangest one was a large, carved, wooden statue with a scary face.

We were staying at the Tradewinds Hotel in Suva in two adjoining rooms. On our first night, I got up to go to the toilet and turned on the bathroom light. Oh my. I froze. Cockroaches were scuttling around everywhere, but not just your standard, house-sized cockroaches. These were the T-Rexes of the cockroach world. After running next door, I pounded on Mum and Dad's door. They were just getting ready for bed. Dad came over, big slipper in hand and started smashing at the insects. He whacked them. They laughed at him, got up, shook a feeler and sauntered off.

Helen and I stood on the bed screaming as the cockroaches decided to leave the comfort of the bathroom under Dad's sustained attack. He ran next door and came back with a new weapon—his hefty, black leather shoe—with Mum as backup. Dad resumed cockroach clobbering while the roaches continued to mock. They were indestructible. Mum took one look at the size of those suckers and demanded that Dad go to reception to get us moved. He marched off in his pyjamas, shoe weapon still in one hand with half a cockroach dangling from it as evidence.

A porter arrived carrying a tin of fly spray. Mum's scowl said it all; she was in no mood for any more nonsense. After a short and abrupt conversation, a housekeeper was dispatched to help us move to a different area of the hotel.

Leaving Fiji I stared sadly out of the plane window. I would miss this island paradise. Mum on the other hand was babbling on about going home to that stupid Lena, the poodle. I turned my attention to my journal and started to write.

Of course everyone was informed in detail of Denise's woefully embarrassing dance moves at the kava ceremony. I shoved my dancing outfit right to the back of the wardrobe, out of sight. I didn't need reminding of that incident.

Dad positioned the weird wooden statue with the creepy face in the living room. Soon after, things started to go wrong: things went missing; things broke; we had car trouble, accidents and bad news.

Mum, Helen and I blamed the Fijian statue. We decided it was possessed and was bringing us bad luck. I've no idea how we jumped to this rash conclusion, but indeed we did. Dad told us not to be ridiculous; he loved it. We waited until he was at work. Mum grabbed the statue, took it out to the garage and tossed it into the bin. Normal life could resume.

1982

NEW ZEALAND

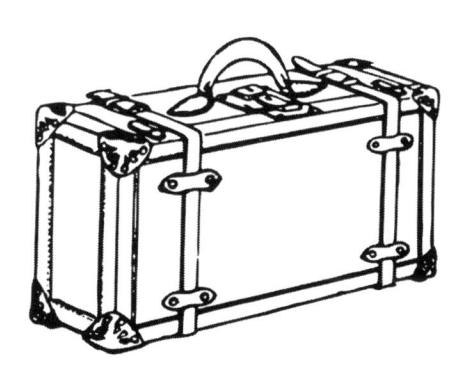

BEINGS, BAPTISTS, BOYS AND A BBQ

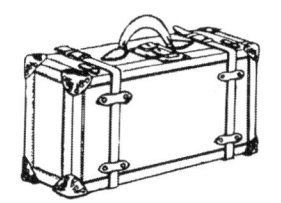

It was July, winter 1982, and the start of the school holidays. Mum, Helen and I were in our little Ford Escort driving up to our bach at Motunau, about an hour and a half's drive from our home in Christchurch. Lena was sitting on Helen's lap in the front passenger seat and I was in the back. Dad had work to do so was going to follow us up a few days later, on the Friday night.

Being the middle of winter, it was already dark as we'd left home after an early dinner at about 6:30 p.m. I shivered in the back seat. Mum cranked the heater up. The night was clear and still. There would be a frost in the early hours. Leaving Christchurch far behind us, we headed into the hilly countryside through Waipara winery country and Omihi farming district. Without light pollution from towns, the night sky full of stars was perfectly illuminated.

After turning off the main road at Greta Valley, we headed out towards the coast, through farmland with just an occasional farmhouse scattered around. As we neared Motunau, there were steep cliffs on our right, dropping straight down to the sea below. Without warning, an enormous, bright, glowing ball of light rose from below the seaward cliffs. It was above the car and to our right. We all saw it at the same time. There was no missing it. The light was huge and intense. This was no star.

'Squid-boat light?' suggested Mum, sounding doubtful.

Squid boats have overhead lights which illuminate the water around them to attract squid. They're fairly stationary and fixed to the vessel. This light was hovering above us and moving at the same speed as the car, keeping pace with us. The hairs stood up on my arms and the back of my neck. Helen leant forward in her seat to gaze upwards, shouting out that the light was above us. Lena let out a low growl.

'It's following us,' screamed Helen.

'It's a UFO,' I called out.

'What's it doing?' yelled Mum, her voice sounding terrified as she tried to concentrate on driving while picturing us all being beamed up by a white light.

'It's staying with us. Drive faster,' Helen shouted.

I felt like crying. We were all on the verge of hysteria. I wished I hadn't read all Dad's UFO books now as I knew exactly what would happen once we were beamed up. Those dreadful, pale aliens with giant, black, saucer eyes would probe us, collect samples then put us on ice. And that was if we were lucky. We were doomed.

Lena growled again. The bright light illuminated the car but just ahead the road dipped, hugging the wall of a vertical escarpment, so we would have some cover. We were coming into Motunau. There were lights on in a few of the bachs, and cars in driveways. Mum slammed her foot on the accelerator and floored it in the old Ford Escort. We tore down the steep road jutting out of the sandstone cliff above the Motunau river. We were almost there.

'It's gone,' shouted Helen with relief.

Mum didn't drive up to our bach as it felt too dark and isolated. Instead she drove into our neighbours' driveway and screeched to a halt next to their house. They were permanent residents at the beach and their lights were all on. We flew from the car and ran to their door. Mum pounded on it until it opened. Without waiting for an invite, we all sprinted into their lounge, a ball of mass hysteria all gibbering at once, visibly trembling.

Joan Bishop looked us up and down, wide-eyed.

'Gordon, you'd best put the kettle on then bring the brandy,' she said, assessing us calmly.

She motioned for us to sit down by the fire to warm up. We all started to speak again. She hushed us and got Mum to explain what had happened while she listened and Gordon passed us each a brandy to sip. We gulped it down then took the hot mugs of tea Joan produced. I noticed them glance at each other with raised eyebrows but nothing was said along the lines of 'are you stark raving mad?' Gordon was dispatched outside for a look around. Not seeing anything, he returned for his car keys and went for a drive around the beach, probably to humour us. When he returned, he of course reported that there was nothing to be seen; it was no doubt just a squid-boat light.

The Bishops again looked at us dubiously. However, they did refrain from calling us nutters, at least until we were out of earshot. Mum moved the car next door and Gordon escorted us inside and put the lights on, without once saying, 'See, no aliens here!' Little did the Bishops know that we hadn't finished with them yet.

Our first week of the school holidays went swimmingly. A notice in our letterbox announced that a Baptist church youth group was setting up a big tent down at the waterfront. There were to be hot toasted sandwiches, tea and coffee for free, and board games and activities throughout the week. Two other girls our age were staying just down the road so Helen and I made friends quickly, as you do at that age, and headed down to the river mouth to check out the youth group. I mean 'check out' literally, as we were teenage girls, and boys were our number one priority. Well, that and toasted sandwiches.

Helen soon found a young man that she liked; he was one of the youth leaders. Another girl with us met a boy so naturally we became a regular fixture. But first we had to get past the religious stuff. Being a sassy fifteen-year-old girl, I wasn't at the time exactly big on tact or religion, so excuse my ignorance. So there I was trying to stuff my face with a cheese and pineapple toasted sandwich (very tasty, by the way) when some guy sat down and tried to convert me. He failed miserably. It went something like this. Bear in mind that my answers were said through cheesy mouthfuls with pineapple juice dribbling out of the corner of my mouth.

Him: 'Do you believe in God?'
Me: 'Nope.'
Him: 'Do you believe in Jesus?'
Me: 'Nope.'

I noticed Helen and the other girls watching the interrogation unfold and sniggering to themselves. They thought it was hilarious that I'd been cornered.

Him: 'Hmmm, have you ever read the Bible?'
Me: 'Are there any more toasted sandwiches? They're so good.'
Him: 'The Bible?'
Me: 'Oh, naa.'
Him: 'If I give you a copy of the Bible, would you like to take it and read it?'
Me: 'Nope.'
Him: 'Would you like to learn more about Christianity?'
Me: 'What? Oh, ah no. I'm just here for the free food.'

He sighed, excused himself and walked away to slump in a seat.

Me: 'Any chance of another toastie?'

Funnily enough he didn't bother me for the rest of the week but I sure did enjoy the free food. We also enjoyed the games of soccer, tag and board games in the company of other young people. It was an excellent idea for the school holidays. Unfortunately it all came to a crashing end. One of the local boys knocked down the big tent one night, tripping in the darkness and pulling all the pegs out of the ground. The church group packed their gear and left in a huff the next day. I was annoyed that my source of free grub had been ripped out from under my feet, literally.

Not to worry, Dad was due that night and Mum was cooking a roast. Yum. Dad settled in and the roast lamb cooking in the oven smelt delicious. While waiting for it to be ready, Helen and I sat close to the little bar heater and filled Dad in on our week of aliens and religious activities. Outside, leaves were quivering in unison, gripping tightly to swaying branches while being pelted with heavy raindrops. The lights suddenly went out. Aww, man, no power meant no roast dinner. Sigh. We assembled torches and candles. Mum turned the oven off and examined the roast. Nope, still raw. We waited a bit to see if the power would come back on. But it didn't and the place was getting cold. Not to worry. Dad had a brainwave. He would bring the BBQ inside to cook tea. Mum had some sausages and the heat from the BBQ would keep us warm as well. That was us sorted.

Dad set up the BBQ in the kitchen of our little open-plan bach and the sausages cooked. We ate dinner and Dad left the BBQ burning until bedtime for warmth, before turning it off. With nothing much to do in the dark, we all went to bed. All three little bedrooms and the bathroom opened off the one rectangular living area. Helen and I closed our bedroom doors and went to sleep.

Sometime later I was woken by a commotion. I could hear Mum wailing, Lena barking and Dad shouting at us girls to come and help. When I stepped into the dimly lit main room, Dad was rushing about in a panic. He said Lena had woken them up barking so Mum had let her out of the kitchen door then promptly fainted on the back doorstep, knocking her face and head. Helen and I went in to see Mum, who Dad had dragged into the bedroom. She was sitting up looking dazed and had a bleeding cut on her face. Helen stayed with her while I headed to the bathroom with a torch to search for the first aid kit in the wall cabinet.

Dad heard an almighty thump and smashing as I hit the deck, out cold. I managed to swipe the entire cabinet contents onto the floor with a sweep of my arm as I went down. He raced in to find patient number two unconscious among an assortment of bathroom products on the floor. Helen was urgently dispatched to fetch help. We had no phone but a nurse lived down the street and our neighbours were home. Dad hooked me under the armpits and began dragging my dead weight across the floor (not helped by all those toasted sandwiches), out into the living room, heading to the couch. Mum was wailing hysterically from the bedroom, feeling too woozy to walk but demanding to know what was going on, and Lena was barking as usual.

Dad's pyjama bottoms chose this point in time to fall down. The elastic had snapped under the strain but he valiantly carried on towards the couch. I picked this moment to come to and open my eyes. I wished I hadn't. The nurse from down the road burst through the door at that precise time and probably wished she hadn't. Thank goodness the power was still out.

They hoisted me onto the couch and Dad quickly yanked his wayward pants up from the floor. Helen arrived with Joan, who brought a big, battery-operated lamp with her. She'd instructed Gordon to boil water on their wood range and to bring cups of tea ASAP. The nurse quickly assessed the situation and, tutting loudly, removed the offending BBQ while Joan opened all the doors and windows, letting fresh, freezing air waft in. My head started to clear. Mum staggered out to sit in the lounge and Dad found his dressing gown. The nurse tended to Mum's wounds and checked us both.

'That wasn't meant to happen,' commented Dad, scratching his head in wonder at the turn of events.

The nurse gave Dad a lecture. Gordon arrived and dispensed cups of steaming tea just in time to hear what the idiot neighbours had done this time: only gone and brought a toxic BBQ into the house and tried to gas themselves to death. 'Irish idiots,' he was probably thinking. Joan was probably wondering if they should move house; somewhere, shall we say, less active.

It turns out that charcoal briquettes emit carbon monoxide, which is of course a toxic, invisible vapour. They're clearly meant for outdoor use only. Indoor BBQs can result in poisoning, unconsciousness or even death. Without smoke, there was no visual sign warning us of the carbon monoxide danger. The only warning we had was that yapping, vicious, snappy little brat of a poodle. Who'd've thought that stupid dog would save the day and be the hero?

Well, that was the first week of the school holidays taken care of: chased by a UFO, attempted religious conversion by the church and nearly gassed to death. I wondered what we would do the following week. Joan announced they were going away for a few days but did enquire as to what date we would be leaving the beach.

Something good did come out of the week spent with the youth group other than dribbling cheese and pineapple. I met a boy. Dan was a handsome-looking lad, sandy-haired, tanned and blue-eyed, from a nearby farming community. He was staying at the beach with his two mates in their parents' bach. He must have been impressed with my communication skills and toastie-eating finesse for after the demise of the tent and, with it, our meeting place, Dan and the two brothers, Todd and Dave, duly knocked on the door of our bach. They asked in an overly formal manner to speak to Dad. Helen and I stood there grinning like Cheshire cats as they asked him if we would be allowed to meet them later that evening. Dad readily agreed, probably thankful for a bit of peace and quiet. Mum and Dad knew the boys' parents so any misbehaving would be reported back and they knew it.

My sister and I were giddy with excitement, choosing our outfits carefully. Luckily I had a brand-spanking-new pale pink and grey jumpsuit that complemented my blonde hair perfectly. It had cost Mum a fortune. I loved it. It was all zips and pockets in a crisp cotton fabric, very Spandau Ballet chic. The appointed time came and Helen and I walked up the hill, full of anticipation. Mum's instructions were ringing in my ears: 'You are *not* to get that new outfit dirty! Do you hear me?'

We arrived at the house the boys were staying in. We talked, laughed and danced the night away to Queen, David Bowie and Joan Jett. Bodies swayed; teenage hearts swooned and my lips locked with

Dan's. The lights went out. The room lit up. Flares of luminescent light showered the room. Todd was smashing open and spraying the place with fluorescent fishing-lure tubes, normally used to attract fish, not girls.

We shrieked and squealed. It looked like a modern-day podium winner spraying the crowd with champagne, only we were being sprayed from head to toe with glowing orange and yellow marine-grade fish-lure lights. I looked down, both horrified and delighted by my fluorescent look. My brand-new outfit was ruined. What on earth would Mum say? It was time to go.

Mum has told this story a million times of how she and Dad were sitting watching out for us. It was dark by then and we had a curfew. Suddenly out of the darkness, skipping down the hill came two glowing skeletons. All that was visible were splatters of luminescent orange and yellow, seemingly disembodied, floating down the hill. 'What the hell is that?' gasped Mum.

They stared, wide-eyed. As the apparitions got closer, the fluorescent skeletons took shape. Mum and Dad could now make out our human forms and clearly hear our giggles as we admired our colourful clothes glowing in the darkness. Our giggling, happy chatter ended abruptly. One look at Mum's face and I knew I was in big trouble. Luckily I was too old for the wooden spoon.

'What have you done to your new outfit?' demanded Mum.

'Umm, that wasn't meant to happen,' I protested.

But she wasn't listening.

'Both of you get your clothes off and into the washing machine right this minute.'

I'm sure I detected a twinkle in Dad's eye as Helen and I raced off to get changed.

Note: The mystery of the UFO was never solved, although the Kaikōura coast was the scene of a well-documented UFO sighting recorded by two pilots in December 1978. I absolutely know that what we saw wasn't a light from a squid boat. I'd seen many squid-boat lights off the coast and this wasn't one of them. We watched the news in the following days for anyone else reporting strange lights but there were no other alleged sightings. I never read another UFO magazine in my life and the story of that week's events became part of our family folklore.

1986

MANCHESTER, NORTHERN IRELAND AND LONDON

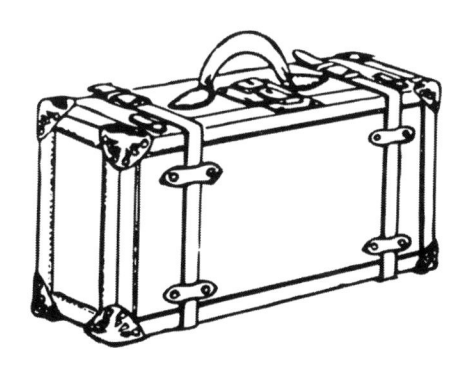

SPOOKY SALFORD SLUM

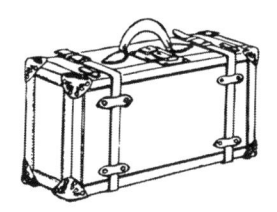

A couple of years after the Motunau saga, I was at college in Christchurch and happily continuing living the life of a clown when Dad said, 'Enough is enough. You're coming to work with me as a receptionist.' So I found myself inhabiting the same office block as my dad, alongside the Ginger Beer Syndicate winners who still couldn't successfully brew ginger beer. But I guess they could afford to buy their own now.

Loosely translated, this job meant fetching important stuff for smoko time, an informal break in New Zealand. I fetched salami, cheese and French bread. I also sent stuff, filed stuff and just did other stuff. The following year, Dad announced, 'We're moving to Wellington and I've sorted you a job in my new office.' He clearly didn't think much of my prospects and there were no current openings for a clown. So receptionist it was. Strangely enough, this job too required a lot of fetching; only being in the capital city, I fetched posher stuff, like pâté.

It was here, while I was a receptionist at a computer company in Wellington, that this long, lanky computer engineer with wavy, sandy hair started hanging out at reception. He draped himself all over my desk, pleading until I relented and went out on a date with him. That was Geoffrey. Dad came home and announced to Mum, 'One of my wizz-kid engineers is sniffing around our Denise.'

On the 22nd of November 1986, Geoffrey and I pulled up in a taxi outside our home for the next month in Salford, Manchester. As we peered out of the window into the grey, dull English light, we saw four steps climbing upwards from the road and a crumbling concrete path that led to the door of an intimidating mansion. Rows of lifeless, bleak windows stood sentinel. Staring up at the building, I shivered. Geoffrey paid the taxi, rummaging around, trying to get to grips with pounds sterling. Yawning, I stretched; jet lag was setting in after our long flights from New Zealand.

This was Geoffrey's first trip overseas and I'd only been to Fiji. So there we were, a pair of novice travellers, alone on the other side of the world, Geoffrey the whizz-kid on an all-expenses-paid working trip to learn about big mainframe computers. And it was only fair that Dad let me go too, given that it was him who'd sent my beloved to the other side of the planet. By switching from hotel to hovel, Geoffrey's daily allowance for accommodation and meals was hopefully going to be enough to cover my being there too. Back home, Dad was celebrating the clown being temporarily off his hands.

We walked towards the dilapidated-looking, red-brick mansion, an imposing, three-storey building that would have been quite grand in its day. Each level had a row of five wooden-sashed windows facing the street. The path took us to a central Roman Doric portico; the date above the door read 1840. With some trepidation, Geoffrey pressed the buzzer; our breath hung in the air while we waited. We could hear footsteps approaching. A stern-looking lady opened the large, creaky door, looked at our proffered bits of paperwork and grabbed a key. She marched off, leading us up an old wooden staircase of immense proportions. Inside was dimly lit and gloomy. Dampness wrapped itself heavily around us.

We scurried to follow her up to the second floor, where she paused ahead of us to unlock a door, showing us into our new home, apartment number 10. She pointed out a shared telephone in the corridor, only for incoming calls. Alarmingly, she showed us a coin meter to put 50p pieces into if we wanted hot water or electricity. Our unsmiling landlady informed us that the small panel heater would come on at strictly set times; for extra heating we would need to feed the meter.

She shut the door behind her, leaving us to look around. As we moved, the wooden floor creaked. Peering out of the window, I immediately felt a cold draught wafting in through gaps around the wooden frames. The wind howled outside and the torn and frayed curtains billowed in the draft. There was no sign of shops in the gathering darkness; our tummies would have to stay hungry. Quickly drawing the curtains across, we shivered; turning the heater on produced only the merest hint of warmth.

The apartment was far from modern. There was no shower in the freezing bathroom off the living area, just an old, green bath tub, pedestal sink and toilet. It looked stark, cold. The main room had a tiny kitchenette, a Formica table and two metal chairs. Two frumpy, brown armchairs and a TV completed the look. A door at the opposite side of the room led to the bedroom. When I flicked the light switch on, a single, dangling lightbulb revealed an old and lumpy double bed covered by a threadbare candlewick bedspread. The stained and yellowing wallpaper was peeling from the walls and a musty smell pervaded. An imposing, dark-wooden wardrobe stood opposite the bed.

It was freezing in the room. Without more 50p pieces, we couldn't heat the water for a bath so we collapsed into bed exhausted, cold and hungry. *Whose dumb idea was this?* I was missing home. I'd never been so far from my family before. It wasn't as if we could even call them; there was no phone for calling out. The only contact we would have with home for the next month would be via letters or if my parents made a toll call to the house number I'd left them.

We were on our own. So this was what it was like being a grown-up; you had to sort shit out for yourself. I was only nineteen and

Geoffrey was twenty-six. Snuggling up for warmth, we drifted off to sleep. Waking suddenly at 4 a.m., we looked around, wondering what had disturbed us. I had a vaguely creepy feeling that we were being watched.

Our thoughts turned to Monday morning, with Geoffrey anxious about starting his course and me nervous about being left alone in a strange place. Feelings of homesickness washed over us.

After eventually drifting back to sleep again in the early hours, we overslept. When I got up to run a bath, I noticed the wardrobe door was standing open. After closing it, I checked to see if it was loose, but it wasn't. Running a shallow, lukewarm bath used up our remaining metered power. When I stepped out of the bathroom, I discovered the heater, lights and fridge all off and Geoffrey sitting enveloped in the old, brown chair, looking glum. Shivering, I wiped the condensation from the window. As I peered outside, I saw people scuttling by, wrapped up in coats, leaning into the rain and wind under leaden skies. Welcome to Manchester in November.

Once we'd wrapped up warmly, we ventured out in search of 50p pieces and food. Next door was a little pub called the Albert Park Inn, and across the road from us was Albert Park sports field. Our new neighbourhood consisted of rows of red-brick, terraced houses and a few older original mansions similar in age to ours. A corner store was located a couple of blocks away where we were able to stock up on 50p pieces and supplies. Back at the apartment, we devoured a lunch of poached eggs on toast washed down with a most welcome cup of English tea.

We spent the afternoon checking out the bus route into Piccadilly station and finding the Arndale Centre where Geoffrey's course was to be held. Later, after discovering the pub was closed, we found ourselves walking the streets in search of somewhere to eat. Heavy rain fell in fluid, silvery curtains, illuminated by the street lamps, sending us dashing back to the spooky, old mansion. Munching on cheese on toast, we watched *EastEnders* while our clothes steadily dripped over the backs of the kitchen chairs. The radiator was stone cold.

A creaking sound disturbed our sleep in the early hours; once again the wardrobe door had opened. Geoffrey got up and slammed it shut, muttering about rickety old furniture, but I felt uneasy. Lying awake, Geoffrey was thinking about his first day on his course while I worried about being alone in a strange city, never mind alone in the creepy apartment. As morning broke, I got up to see Geoffrey off, sharing breakfast and a hot cup of tea with him before he left. The window steamed up with my breath as I watched him forlornly from our draughty sash window while he walked down the path.

A shallow, icy bath shocked me into wakefulness. Wrapped up warmly, I faced the world alone, setting off apprehensively back to the corner store for some provisions and more 50p pieces. I found myself confused with the unfamiliar English coins and the shopkeeper's Salford accent. You wouldn't think we were both speaking English.

After lunch I crouched over the bathtub, laboriously handwashing all our dirty clothes, then got inventive in finding places to drape them. I clicked the TV on and flopped onto one of the ugly, brown armchairs, nodding off as jet lag caught up with me. A loud bang jolted me awake as the bedroom door suddenly flew shut. Heart pounding, I went to investigate but knew that no one else should be in the apartment. Of course no one was there. Silly really; surely it was just the wind?

I was relieved when Geoffrey returned home at 5:30 p.m. and we escaped next door to our new local pub for a couple of hours. The warmth of the cosy bar and being surrounded by other people was most welcome.

'D'you think there's a ghost in the apartment?' I asked.

'Undoubtedly. You're not content with just attracting aliens; you've now moved on to ghosts,' replied Geoffrey, sipping his ale.

'It's got nothing to do with me,' I snapped. 'It's not my fault there's a ghost living in our wardrobe.'

'You reckon,' muttered Geoffrey. 'No wonder your dad wanted you off his hands for a bit.'

While I was cooking dinner a couple of days later, ironically lamb chops from New Zealand, the landlady suddenly pounded on the door, shouting that there was a phone call for me. She told me to pick up the phone on the landing; it was Mum. After listening to Mum speak, I felt my voice quavering but refrained from telling her the flat was a slum run by Miss Frosty Knickers and shared with a closet ghost.

As I sat in bed later, I finished my diary by torchlight, misty breath hanging in the air. Geoffrey and I had been watching TV earlier when the coins ran out, plunging us into darkness. So there we were in bed, with no lights and no heat. This wasn't how I'd imagined a glamorous trip to the UK might be.

I spent my time exploring Great Clowes Street and further afield around Manchester, shopping for Christmas gifts at the Arndale Centre, cooking, cleaning and scrubbing clothes over the bathtub. Arriving home one day, I found a letter from Mum and Dad shoved under our apartment door. When I tore it open, hungry for news from home, I chuckled at their complaints about the hot weather and talk of Christmas BBQs. I finished reading the letter then read it all over again before wandering over to gaze wistfully across the road at Albert Park and the children happily playing soccer. BANG. The bedroom door slammed shut with force. As I jumped in fright, a cold chill ran down my spine. I nervously approached the doorway to the bedroom and peeped in. There was nothing there and no wind. It was time for a cup of tea.

Geoffrey and I spent our evenings next door at the homely Albert

Park Inn, where our faces became familiar to the bar staff and locals. They always greeted us with, 'Here come those funny-talking Kiwis.' The so-called entertainment was always interesting; it would seem that most of the pub's regulars considered themselves talented singers. The talent was both delightful and dreadful at the same time. Apart from this splendid entertainment, the main attraction was that it was warm and we were saving 50p coins while sampling British beers.

On Fridays, Geoffrey finished his course at lunchtime, collecting a rental car on his way home, where I eagerly awaited him with bags ready and waiting. We spent our weekends exploring the Lake District, Scotland, Wales, Oxford, Devon and the Cotswolds. We marvelled at the history, wandering around historical sights, monuments, castles, dungeons and stone circles, all with a sense of wonder. Everything was so ancient and with a sense of timelessness and mystery that we just don't have at home in New Zealand.

Partway through our stay in Manchester, I left Geoffrey to his course and the ghostie to his wardrobe to head off on my own adventure.

THE RED WITCHES OF BELFAST

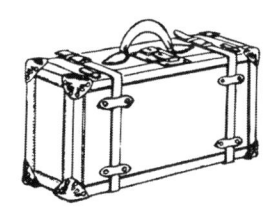

One day in early December, Geoffrey finished his course a little earlier to escort me in the taxi to Manchester Airport. I was off to Belfast, Northern Ireland, to meet my Irish family for the first time. I'd been writing letters to my aunt Addie since I was about eight years old. She was actually my great-aunt but known simply as Aunt Addie, and I loved her. We shared the same birthday and she came from my father's birthplace—Ireland—a long, long way from New Zealand. I'm not sure what she made of these persistent letters she'd been receiving from a child in New Zealand for the last ten years but to me she was special and I couldn't wait to meet her. According to my dad, he was her favourite nephew. I'd seen photos of course but soon I would be meeting her in person, as well as her daughters, Nora, the oldest, who was 31 and Pauline who was 25.

This was Northern Ireland at the time of The Troubles so security was tight around all flights to Belfast. Dad had instructed me not to mention the company I worked for as they were British. Geoffrey's course in Manchester also had strict security measures in place because of bomb threats. At the airport, passengers flying to Belfast were separated into a different area to all other passengers for rigorous searches. Everyone travelling to Northern Ireland had to fill out extra documentation. Armed police were highly evident, even out on the tarmac as I boarded the plane. This was disconcerting to a young girl from a gun-free New Zealand travelling alone for the first time.

After the short flight to Belfast, I nervously found my way into the baggage-collection area. While the other passengers were greeted with warm smiles and hugs, I was left unclaimed. With my bag in hand, I anxiously looked around, wondering what to do next. Everyone dispersed, leaving me behind. As I stood on the cold white tiles, the room fell silent apart from the echo of retreating footsteps.

A set of large swinging doors to the side flew open and the room was suddenly filled with the sound of laughter. Rushing towards me was my aunt Addie, tall, willowy, grey-haired and beautiful. Strong arms embraced me before I was enveloped by hugs from Pauline, her thick, blonde hair escaping from under her winter hat. Brushing her sister aside, tall, slim and dark-haired Nora seized me in a warm embrace before introducing me to her partner, Len. We all squeezed into Len's little hatchback for the drive home to Rosebery Gardens, the very address that I'd been posting letters to for ten years. I was eager to see the house in person.

It was a traditional, two-up, two-down, brick terraced house with a small square of garden in front and a little square of garden out the back. Downstairs, we entered the front room; the kitchen and laundry were at the rear of the house. As I discovered the next day, the tiny back garden held more gnomes or leprechauns than plants. The place was just perfect—perfectly Irish, perfectly quirky.

The cider, wine, laughter and conversation flowed with no awkwardness. I knew these people; they were me; they were my people, my Irish family and I loved them all. I felt at home. Finally, people as silly as me. I fitted right in. They opened their Christmas presents from New Zealand with great excitement and pored over photos from home. Wearily I crept upstairs in the early hours to the back bedroom (normally Pauline's). Aunt Addie was opposite me in the front bedroom, sharing with Pauline, and a bathroom was across the landing. After climbing into the soft bed, under a warm pile of duvets, I lay staring into the darkness. I found it hard to believe I was finally there. This house had been in the family for many years and had seen a lot of life within these walls.

When I got up next day, Pauline had left for work already so I had breakfast with Aunt Addie then the two of us went for a stroll, arm in arm, to the local shops. I don't think she needed anything; she just wanted to show off her New Zealand visitor. The Irish people were ever so friendly with a great sense of community. Everyone knew each other and had time for a chat. Aunt Addie led me around to Imperial Street, where my dad grew up, taking photos of me standing proudly outside his old front door.

After lunch, Len and Nora called by for us. He'd taken the day off work specially as no one else in the family owned a car. Like many people in Belfast at this time, they were struggling financially so I was touched by their kindness. Our chauffeur drove us to the pretty seaside towns of Bangor and Helen's Bay. These were special places to my dad and grandparents that I'd heard them talk about with great fondness as they remembered family holidays.

The stories continued back at Aunt Addie's, where I was introduced to red witches, a drink made by mixing Pernod, cider and blackcurrant juice. When Pauline arrived home from work, Len, Nora, she and I went out for dinner. Once seated in the restaurant, they began asking me questions about life in New Zealand. My cousins had been living through the horror of The Troubles throughout their entire lifetimes; they'd never known a time of peace. The IRA (Irish Republican Army) was fighting the British security forces over Northern Ireland's independence. Then religion got tangled up in it all—Catholic versus Protestant—with disastrous results. Hearing my family's stories made me appreciate my home even more.

Later that night the phone rang; Geoffrey was calling me, lonely in the spooky old mansion. He was continuing to experience early morning awakenings, finding the wardrobe door open. I was grateful for my cosy ghost-free room where the wardrobe held only clothes.

I went out with Pauline and Nora the following day, doing a bit of Christmas shopping followed by a bit of cider drinking. Apparently Christmas shopping in Belfast was just code for drinking the afternoon away. I was surprised when armed guards searched my bags at the entrance to large department stores, small reminders that all was not right there. Our trio savoured every moment together, revelling in each other's company and merrily laughing over old stories, or perhaps that was the cider talking. The next entry from my journal was without doubt cider talk as it says, and I quote:

'They want me to come back next year with Dad and Nana to go sailing with a few bottles of rum and cider.'

What? Where did that come from? None of us could even sail a boat. Hell, I don't think any of us could swim, for that matter. And sail where? The Irish Sea? It was obviously good cider we were drinking. Mind you, our Irish family does have a nautical history. One of my grandad's uncles had famously built a boat in Belfast. He spent over a year carefully crafting a wooden vessel ready to sail the high seas. There was just one problem—the daft beggar built it up in his attic without a thought for how he was going to get a bloody great boat down the stairs and out of the front door. For all I know, somewhere in Belfast sits a house with a large boat wedged in its attic to this day. That we're from such daft lineage as this perhaps sheds some light on the rest of us.

When we returned safely, and a little pie-eyed from shopping, dear aunt Addie greeted us with Irish stew for supper. We'd just started to sober up when Pauline's fiancé, Shaun, arrived. More ciders were poured, oh dear. He was a charming bloke who obviously thought the world of Pauline. Shaun was working at labouring jobs and money was tight. He perfectly complemented Pauline's long, thick head of blonde hair and pale Irish complexion with his dark-black, wavy hair. Len arrived after work and our inebriated little group sat down to watch Pauline's favourite Christmas movie, *Frosty the Snowman*, though you'll forgive me if my memory is sketchy. I think I could see two or three Frosties by then. Group photos were taken, everyone happy, everyone smiling or laughing and all of us 100 per cent sloshed.

Lord, have mercy on my head was all I could think upon stepping out of bed next morning. It was fine and cold at noon as Aunt Addie, Nora, Pauline and I set off for a walk through Ormeau Park near Rosebery Gardens. Out the other side of the gated park, we visited Dunnes Stores. But before my fuddled head knew what was happening, I found myself sitting in Molly's Pub, quaffing Castaway Wine Cooler all afternoon. At 5 p.m. our motley crew of Castaway-soaked sailor wannabes lurched out of the pub, only to find the gate to the park had been locked. We had to stumble home arm in arm the long way.

One glance at the clock on Aunt Addie's mantlepiece in the front room confirmed the worst. We were by now running horribly late for getting me to the airport on time. Len had to work so we didn't have the car. Aunt Addie rustled up some mince on toast which we quickly devoured. Unbelievably (except if you're Irish) this unstoppable band of merry Irish maidens mixed a fresh batch of red witches to wash down the mince. While I sat dazed at the kitchen table, Aunt Addie somehow managed to order a taxi and throw my stuff in the suitcase. Well, at least I think she did. I have no recollection of the taxi ride but apparently it took us to the bus depot. From there our merry troupe boarded the bus to Belfast Airport.

As we sat down, I heard the unmistakable sound of bottles clinking. What? Surely not? Unbelievable! Aunt Addie and Nora quickly produced four glasses, a bottle of Pernod, a bottle of cider and another of blackcurrant juice out of their voluminous handbags and began mixing up red witches as if this was a perfectly normal thing to do. I watched, wide-eyed. Were they trying to get us thrown off the bus? Pauline was slumped in her seat and giggled shrilly.

Other passengers stared at us in disbelief. I nervously glanced towards the driver; I could see his eyes watching us in the rear-view mirror.

It wasn't long before the red witches worked their magic, erasing my fears. All I could do was proffer a tipsy grin. Every time we went over a bump, our bright-red drinks went flying. Aunt Addie's wispy, grey hair had come adrift and her flushed cheeks were as red as the drink in her hand. She was hanging tightly onto the seat in front for support with one hand, glass in the other. Nora was giddy, swaying and glassy-eyed, Pauline still grinning absently. We were blotto, blitzed. *Will we get kicked off the bus?* I wondered. It wouldn't be the first time for me but I had a plane to catch.

'What's the story?' shouted the bus driver.

Aunt Addie loudly, and with the merest hint of a slur, informed him and the entire busload of passengers.

'Our Denissssee is from New Zealand. We're seeing her off with a wee craic at the airport.'

After a moment's thoughtful silence, he replied, 'Grand. I'll be along after my shift for a bit of the black stuff.'

I relaxed back in my seat, sipping at the surprise onboard refreshments, relieved that the imminent threat of being kicked off the bus was gone.

With my bag checked in, we found my flight had been delayed by a couple of hours. Relief washed over me that I hadn't missed it and would have some time to sober up. Aunt Addie hooked her surprisingly strong arm through mine and ushered us into the nearest bar. My liver recoiled involuntarily. A drink was shoved in my hand. Time passed in a boozy blur. Things were starting to look a little hazy.

I was startled by a booming voice and a hearty thump on the shoulder. A pair of big, black boots stood before me. Looking up with bleary eyes, I saw the bus driver, still in his uniform, looming over me. For a moment I had a flashback to another bus driver, another pair of boots and crabs running around the floor, but nope, no crabs here. Squinting, I could see his name badge now; it said Pat. The driver promptly bought another round of drinks to loud cheers and applause.

My legs had developed a decided wobble. The room may have been spinning slightly; I'm not sure on that one.

Someone among us must have been savvy enough to keep an eye on the flight departures board for suddenly I was being bodily supported to the gate, leaning heavily on our burly bus driver. We all started to cry, even the silly driver who, until a few hours earlier, didn't know me from a bar of soap. Hugs were dished out aplenty. And while giving me a final, tearful, booze-induced embrace, Pat promised me he would drive Aunt Addie, Nora and Pauline home in his bus, right to their front door. *Wait. What? So is his bus sitting outside somewhere? Is he technically still on duty? Surely he should have returned his bus to the depot? Are there passengers dotted around Belfast, patiently waiting for the airport bus to arrive? So many questions, never to be answered*, I thought as I staggered through the gate.

And this is how, on that crisp winter's night, a merry band of Irish maidens, still swigging on their red witches, rode through the town's streets on a wayward airport bus. They were delivered right to their door at Roseberry Gardens by our Christmas angel in big, black boots. As the noisy bus pulled up and the door opened with the familiar pppsssttt sound, three ladies tumbled out, net curtains twitched and Pat yelled out, 'Merry Christmas,' before driving away in the big, red bus.

Painfully I opened one eye and then the other, looking around. I was back in the Salford slum. *How did I get here?* Surely I couldn't have forgotten an entire flight, let alone arriving at the other end. I called out for Geoffrey; my voice was hoarse. I needed water so I staggered out of bed. The wardrobe door was open.

'And don't even think about starting with me today,' I shouted, slamming the wardrobe door, wincing as pain shot through my head.

Geoffrey wasn't in the apartment and it looked like a bombshell had hit it; luggage and parcels were strewn all over the show. After three cups of coffee, as I sat slumped in the brown chair, I started to have flashbacks. I could recall someone wearing big, black boots; there was a bus and there were red witches.

As I slowly unpacked, I came across bottles of Castaway Wine Cooler. My stomach lurched and I ran for the bathroom. Staring at my reflection in the bathroom mirror, I noticed one of my best earrings was missing. I groaned as I started to piece together the previous night's events. But how the heck did I get back to the apartment and how did Geoffrey get me up the stairs?

He filled in the blanks when he got home.

'You were a disgrace!'

'Fair play,' I responded facetiously.

Geoffrey and I just had one last week before we left Salford. *That should be long enough to recover*. I wouldn't be sorry to say goodbye to the apartment or its spooky resident, that was for sure.

SEND IN THE CLOWNS

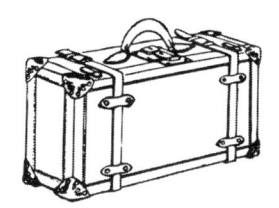

It was time to pack; we were leaving Salford and our prestigious apartment to head to London for a couple of nights before our flight departed from Heathrow, homeward bound. Geoffrey arrived with the hire car and managed to wrestle our bulging suitcases into it. With a last look around our bleak apartment, we slammed the wardrobe door shut and returned the keys to Miss Frosty Knickers. Looking up as we pulled away from the curb, I could have sworn I saw the curtain move in our bedroom window. I shuddered. *Probably just a draft.* Leaving Salford behind on a cold, wintry day, we headed for London.

Our destination was Essex, where we would be staying with Geoffrey's cousin Will and his wife, Rachel, for a couple of nights. But first we were all to rendezvous at the oldies' house for a slap-up dinner of good old English bangers and mash with plenty of gravy; the oldies being Will's parents. Everyone met us there after work: Will, Rachel, and Will's brother Tom. After dinner we young ones set off for a pub about half an hour's drive away. Our hosts were keen to show us a traditionally warm Essex welcome and we were to meet the third of this trio of Hayhurst brothers there. Will went ahead; Rachel was next in her car, followed by us. Tom was left bringing up the rear in his vehicle, in case we got lost; a convoy of Hayhursts.

We were driving along the main road heading out of Essex in icy conditions, the heater turned to high. The street lights revealed a park on one side and a row of buildings to our right. Without warning, a sports car pulled out of a side street ahead of us, straight in front of Rachel, narrowly avoiding a collision. The driver of the car swerved hard, locking the brakes. The sports car skidded, sliding towards Geoffrey and me. Geoffrey braked hard and tried to swerve but our vehicle had no grip on the icy road. The sports car did a full spin, its rear bumper smashing into the front of our car. There was a deafening bang accompanied by the grating sound of crunching metal and glass. The car glanced off our bonnet, mounted the curb and came to rest in the park, smoke billowing from under its bonnet.

The impact brought our vehicle to a shuddering halt, throwing us forward against the strain of our seat belts. As we sat there stunned and dazed, it felt like time had temporarily stood still. My neck hurt and we were shaken but other than that, we thankfully seemed to be in one piece. *That wasn't meant to happen*, I thought as we hastily clambered out of the car.

The poor boy driving the other car suddenly found himself at the centre of a Hayhurst maelstrom as our convoy surrounded him accusingly. Rachel, probably in shock, was loudly hurling abuse at him. Quite apart from the unlikely scenario of having four cars of Hayhursts as witnesses, things were about to take an entirely stranger turn.

Without warning, three clowns suddenly stepped forwards from the shadows of the park. Rachel paused, mid-rant, a surprised look on her face. I took an involuntary step backwards. Everyone fell silent. All eyes were focused on the clowns, bodies tensed lest we should need to run. I was thankful they weren't carrying red balloons and calling for

Georgie (but I jest; the film *It* was years away in the future). The lead clown—let's call him Pennywise—addressed Rachel.

'Aite, babes, chill, bit of a beef goin' on, innit.'

We all exhaled. They weren't here to suck us down the nearest watery drain. Clowns one, two and three had witnessed the accident from where they lurked, doing whatever clowns do in the darkness. *Is someone going to ask them about their clownness?* I wondered. Yes, they were. Will spoke up and asked the obvious. 'Why are you lot dressed like clowns?'

Clown number two spoke. 'We're off to a bit of a do, fancy dress, like, an' saw this eejit land in the bushes.'

That was funny, I thought, grabbing my coat out of the car. It was freezing out and I was starting to shiver. A police officer arrived from across the road. *Where did he materialise from?* I wondered as no police car had pulled up. Glancing to the right gave me the answer. Why, of course, the crash just happened to be right outside a police station; how convenient. The police officers on duty had heard the loud bang and someone had come to investigate.

'Feds are 'ere,' announced clown number three, shuffling his feet and looking nervous.

Possibly a good idea he's in disguise.

Another police officer appeared to help take statements and keep the peace as Rachel, Will and Tom were becoming animated with the perpetrator. There was no point arguing; he didn't stand a chance against this lot. It took the police officers a few minutes to gain control and take notes. One of them summed it all up with a shake of his head and a roll of his eyes. 'So the victim is Geoffrey Hayhurst, whose rental car was hit by this gentleman.' He gave a cursory nod towards the young male driver. 'The other three witness cars are all driven by Hayhursts and the secondary witnesses are three clowns. Is that correct?'

'Sick,' responded Pennywise, nodding his head, red wig tilting to one side.

'Yes, sir,' replied Geoffrey on behalf of team Hayhurst.

'And one last question. Are the clowns related to you also?'

'No, sir, they're just random clowns,' replied Geoffrey.

After taking phone numbers from the clowns and getting all the details for insurance, we collected some pieces of our rental car off the road, shoved them on the back seat and drove on to the pub. We were still in a convoy, only this time our poor car was a bit beaten up and had one headlight hanging out.

Meanwhile waiting anxiously for us all at the pub was number three Hayhurst brother, Michael, and a friend of his. They were beginning to wonder what had happened to us. The tale of the car crash, the Hayhurst mob, Rachel's temper and the three clowns was retold over a drink and many laughs. Later we headed back to Will and Rachel's Essex abode.

We spent two days enjoying the company of our convivial hosts and being treated to the great British tradition of Sunday lunch, followed by a stroll to the corner pub. Snow greeted us on our final morning as we sat drinking our steaming cups of coffee and looking out to the back garden. It looked like a winter wonderland, complete with two delightful squirrels dashing about. The topic of conversation while listening to the BBC weather report revolved around the chances of a white Christmas. We, on the other hand, would be flying home to a Kiwi Christmas with sunshine, sunscreen and sunglasses. After a hearty cooked breakfast, we said a fond farewell to our newly acquainted family members before driving to Heathrow to deliver our now battle-scarred rental car and fly home.

After a circuitous route around the planet via Dubai, Perth, Sydney and Auckland, we were on our final flight home to Wellington on Christmas Eve afternoon. The pilot interrupted my festive daydreams to announce that we would be experiencing some turbulence on the approach to landing. The Christmas fairy lights in my head were abruptly extinguished, replaced by the flashing 'Fasten Seat Belt' sign blinking with urgency. Wellington is known as the windy city, and not without reason. I looked across at Geoffrey for support. His head hung forward, jaw relaxed, skin drooping, while he snorted softly in his sleep, much like he had been for the entire flight.

'Shit,' I blurted as the plane lurched. Grabbing hold of the hand rests, I gripped them tightly, breaking out in a hot sweat as the plane was tossed around in the sky. It seemed as if every nut, bolt and screw was being shaken loose. I tried to remember the brace position. Geoffrey snored peacefully.

Just as we were approaching the runway, a violent crosswind caught the plane, turning it almost side-on. My eyes bulged; shit, this wasn't good. The pilot had a split second to make a decision—ram the plane down and get home for Christmas turkey or abort. He chose the turkey. Gunning the engines he hit the tarmac with such force that we briefly bounced right back up again. Geoffrey's eyes popped wide open. The plane crashed down with a thud, rocking at an alarming angle as we slalomed at force, a giant missile speeding towards the ocean at the other end of the runway. Geoffrey yawned and stretched. I gripped, sweated and swore. The pilot wrested control. I remembered to breathe. We were home. Welcome to windy Wellington. I glared across at Geoffrey.

'What?' he asked.

1988

AUSTRALIA

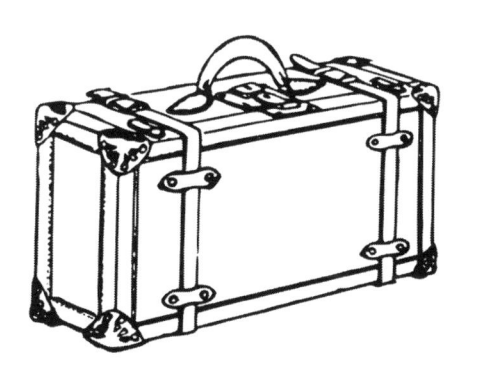

HEAT, HUNTSMAN AND HORSES

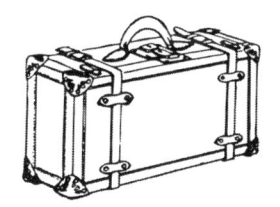

*D*ad had set his sights on Geoffrey taking the clown off his hands for good and had enthusiastically given me away to be married in March 1987. In fact he was so enthusiastic that he began celebrating before the ceremony in true Irish style. Running late and a little tipsy, we arrived at the wrong function room. After opening the double doors with a grand flourish, Dad and I eagerly entered the room. It fell silent as all eyes turned to look at us in surprise.

'Who the hell are these people?' Dad whispered.

'It's the wrong wedding.' I gasped. The universe spluttered and we hastily exited.

The following year, as a 21-year-old, I took my first steps further away from home by moving to Melbourne, Australia. Geoffrey and I were embarking on an exciting new adventure as young newlyweds. We'd left our lives, family and friends behind in New Zealand to follow our latest opportunity. Geoffrey had been offered a transfer to their Melbourne office by the company we both worked for, with relocation costs included. How could we refuse? We had to leave our precious, rough-coated collies with my parents until we could find a rental that would take the dogs too. Mum waved us off at the airport, putting on a brave face. She told me later that she cried all the way home.

Geoffrey settled into his new job and we both enjoyed exploring Melbourne city and its surrounds while staying in an apartment in Toorak near the city centre. We came to love the city, with its green spaces divided by the Yarra River snaking through the middle of town. The turn-of-the-century architecture and colourful green and yellow trams crisscrossing the city were charming. Melbourne proved itself to be a multi-cultural place, a foodie's delight, with plentiful markets, sophisticated shopping, arts and culture.

A few weeks later, we answered an ad in the newspaper for an old, weatherboard villa at Black Rock on the Mornington Peninsula. The house was ultimately destined for demolition; hence dogs weren't an issue. We secured our tenancy and settled into our new home with our two dogs who were flown over to join us.

What stands out from my memories of Melbourne is the intense heat. We were unprepared for our first experience of summer in Australia. The house wasn't built for high temperatures; lacking in insulation, she soaked up the heat like a sponge. Our golden oldie was missing hot-climate necessities like air-conditioning, ceiling fans, tiled floors and high ceilings. She did however have smart black and white striped canvas awnings that pulled down over the windows to keep the sun out. I didn't understand this concept as you were then left in semi-darkness for the summer months.

Our first heatwave hit and 43 sultry degrees for a week sapped us of energy, leaving us in a sweaty stupor. We were a couple of sissies from windy Wellington and this was a shock. In the darkened lounge, I sat with my feet in a bucket of water and a wet flannel on my head. Whoosh, whoosh, whoosh whirred the fan. Smack and splat went the fly swatter. This wasn't how I'd imagined life in Australia would be.

The neighbours had a pool. I knew this because I poked my eye up to the teeny gap in the fence to stare at it longingly. Crisp blue tiles and sparkling clean water were tantalisingly close. Hanging the washing out and swatting at flies, I listened with envy to the inviting trickle of pool water running through the pump, or rhythmic strokes as the elderly couple swam lengths. I headed back across the crunchy brown grass, returning to my bucket, flannel and the whoosh of the fan.

Occasionally we went for a drive in the car just to cool off with the air-con on. That was until we discovered something else typically Australian—the huntsman spider and its love of cars. As we drove back to our house one day, suitably chilled by the air-con, I noticed a movement out of the corner of my eye above Geoffrey's head. A monstrous, hairy huntsman spider, not much smaller than a dinner plate, scuttled across the car ceiling above us. I let rip with a holler loud enough to convey a mortal and imminent threat to life.

Geoffrey, looking completely flummoxed, swerved the car over to the curb as I made a bid for freedom out of the moving vehicle.

'What?' demanded Geoffrey.

As I leapt out, hyperventilating, I pointed at the ceiling, lost for words. Geoffrey looked up, shouted, 'F#@%,' and swiftly exited.

We decided to walk home. Geoffrey bravely returned, armed with fly spray, but the hairy huntsman had done a Houdini and was never seen again.

Later in the summer, Geoffrey and I visited a wildlife park in rural Victoria where you could roam about with the kangaroos and wallabies. One thing about Geoffrey and animals: he can't read the signals, signs, body language, call it what you will, not a clue. So of course he chose to hand-feed a particularly large male kangaroo, which I could clearly see from a distance was not the friendliest roo in the zoo. It wanted the food but not the human contact.

Its ears were twitching and its tail started to thump. It had had enough of this pesky human and anyone could see that. But instead of backing off, Geoffrey persisted, unaware. Suddenly the kangaroo reared up and, whack, it took a right hook with its front leg towards Geoffrey's chin.

He had the reflexes to dodge it; that in itself was a surprise because if he could predict that happening, how come he couldn't predict that the darned thing was getting annoyed? So what did Geoffrey do? He took an air shot right back towards its face. The kangaroo froze with a look of startled disbelief, as if asking itself, 'Did that stupid human really just pretend to thump me?' It recovered and came at him with a left hook. Geoffrey again dodged and wasn't sure whether to smack it or run for his life. The kangaroo had two choices: turn really vicious and disembowel this drongo or depart gracefully as this human was clearly unhinged. And the latter is what it did; hence Geoffrey is still here to tell the tale and I still shake my head in disbelief. Geoffrey gained a new respect for the Australian kangaroo.

In Melbourne we had regular visitors from home to keep us from being too homesick but I found it hard not seeing my parents. Mum and Dad flew over for a much-anticipated visit after we'd been there for twelve months. One day while Geoffrey was at work, Mum, Dad and I headed into Melbourne using public transport for a day's shopping. Dad was only with us to keep an eye on Mum's spending. After leaving home we walked towards Black Rock shops to catch the bus to the train station. Despite the early hour, the cicadas were already singing, the air still and humid.

Once we'd arrived at Melbourne's central railway station, we caught a tram. Hopping off in Toorak, Mum's excitement was building and so was Dad's blood pressure when he saw the prices. Mum went mad in the shops and Dad went mad at her for going mad in the shops. We were so laden down with parcels, we could barely walk. It was time to go. After hailing a cab to the train station, three weary shoppers sat in the back seat, Dad grumbling and fingering his credit card nervously, Mum grinning with satisfaction at a job well done.

Once we'd caught the train and a bus back to Black Rock shops, we were as spent as Dad's credit card but we still had to face the walk home along blistering pavements, lugging all the bags.

'Wait here,' said Mum. 'I just need to get something.' And she ducked into the hardware store.

Dad and I stood sweating in the shade of the building, the concrete radiating heat. Finally Mum re-emerged, triumphantly carrying a broom, a big yard broom, to be precise.

'Oh, for goodness' sake,' I muttered.

Dad and I stared at the broom in surprise. Had she lost her mind in the heat? *Great. Now we have something else to try and lug back home.* Dad was clearly irritated and opened his mouth to resume grumbling. Ignoring him, Mum shoved the bristly end in my hands and got Dad to hold the other end as if we were about to have a game of sidewalk limbo. Then, in what was to be known as Mum's finest hour, she began threading each of the shopping bags onto the broomstick.

'There,' said Mum triumphantly. 'Now we're ready.'

'Mum, you're a complete genius,' I said.

Even Dad was impressed. This was way easier to carry. So off we set through the streets of Black Rock, single file, Dad at the front holding one end of the broom and me bringing up the rear with the bristly end. The bags of shopping hung evenly distributed along the length of the broom between us. The sight of our unique transportation system caused a few laughs and friendly catcalls but we didn't care. As we walked down our street, shopping bags loftily swaying from a pole, I noticed a few neighbours staring at us from their mansions. Our chances of ever getting an invitation to the neighbours' pool were now about zero.

Melbourne Cup rolled around in November towards the end of our first year in Australia. The cup that stops a nation, it's Australia's most famous thoroughbred horse race, held on the first Tuesday in

November. It's a huge occasion, celebrated with a lot of champagne, drinking, fancy hats, fashion, strawberries and of course a horse race.

I was now working at Data General and had become friends with my colleagues on the helpdesk, including Cheryl who was a few years older than me, tall and slim with curly, brown hair. She was outgoing and friendly with a cheeky personality. With a similar sense of humour, we hit it off right away. Geoffrey and I were invited around to celebrate Cup Day at Cheryl and her husband Pete's house where we enjoyed a traditional Australian BBQ dinner accompanied by flowing champagne, wine and beer. Much later, when it got dark, we retreated inside. Pete produced his finest whisky. Cheryl and I declined. The merriment and sun made Geoffrey woozy (you could call it boozy) and he had to go and lie down in our host's spare room. We'd discussed walking into town to go dancing so Cheryl, Pete and I chatted while waiting to see if Geoffrey revived. He didn't, so we decided the three of us would go while leaving Geoffrey to sleep it off.

However, by then our decision-making abilities had degenerated somewhat and Pete, an ex-paramedic, had reverted to his medical training.

'But what if Geoffrey chokes on his vomit while we're out?' he asked with grave concern. While we ignored the fact that no vomiting was happening, Geoffrey was innocently sleeping, unaware of imminent invasion.

A plan was hatched, largely by the inebriated Pete. We would creep into the spare room and check Geoffrey's airways were clear before we departed for the dance club. Pete fetched his medic's bag and gloved up. We opened the door as quietly as three drunks possibly could, then Pete crept in, followed by Cheryl and me. The bedroom was dark. Pete led the way, tiptoeing to the bed, Cheryl and I following, trying to stifle giggles.

Pete located his patient lying on his back snoring happily, but concerned for a possible problem with Geoffrey's airways, Pete rolled him swiftly onto his side into the recovery position and ordered Cheryl and me to position Geoffrey's knee forward to support him. Geoffrey's sozzled form snuffled and grunted then resumed snoring.

Pete flicked his rubber glove menacingly then moved in. He tilted Geoffrey's head back by grabbing a tuft of his hair with one hand and pulling it upwards; his other hand pulled Geoffrey's lower jaw down. In shot Pete's big-gloved finger, probing all around Geoffrey's mouth, poking clumsily down the back of his throat to make sure it was clear of any chunks.

'Ouch,' screamed Pete.

Geoffrey had chomped down, his gag reflex waking him with a jolt. He sat bolt upright with a look of horror on his face. (I can't say I blame him, waking to a stranger's finger probing his oral cavity.) Geoffrey gagged violently, caused by the finger almost down his oesophagus. We all leapt back as a jet of vile vomit was forcibly ejected from Geoffrey's mouth all over the floor.

'Oh Jeez,' said Cheryl.

'That wasn't meant to happen,' muttered Pete. 'I told you it wasn't safe to leave him,' he announced, feeling vindicated.

We three night-time bedroom bandits quickly retreated out of the room. Geoffrey bolted for the bathroom. We weren't popular, I can tell you, and unsurprisingly Geoffrey and I were never again invited to Cheryl and Pete's house.

After we'd been living in Australia for a couple of years, Geoffrey's younger brother Gavin moved to Melbourne on the first stage of his overseas experience, when young Kiwis and Aussies head to Europe after graduating from university or college to work and travel for a year or two. It was great to have some family nearby again and also highly convenient. We handed him our keys and left him in charge of the house and dogs while we visited Canada and Alaska.

Geoffrey and I remained in Melbourne for four years before returning to New Zealand to raise a family of our own closer to home.

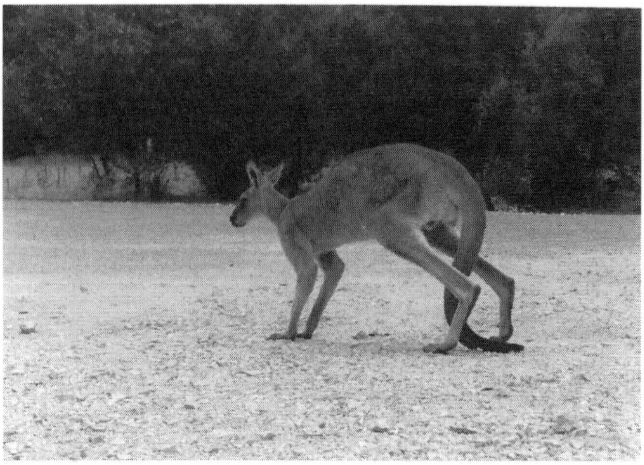

1990

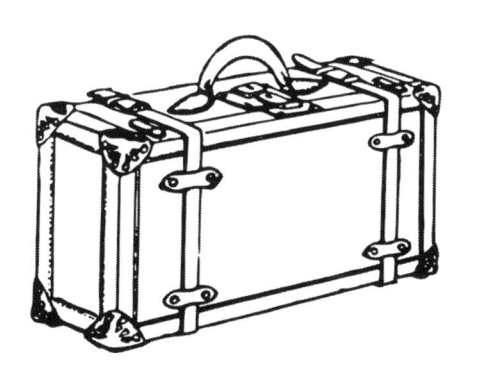

CANADA

CUSTOMS AND COOKING

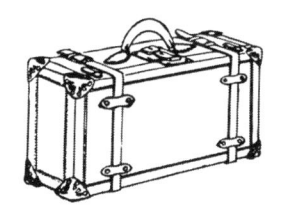

With Gavin looking after our dogs, Geoffrey and I flew to Vancouver, planning a road trip around British Columbia, the Yukon and Alaska in an RV (recreational vehicle or campervan).

Long-haul flights are my worst nightmare and the one from New Zealand to Los Angeles and then on to Vancouver had been no exception. When we stopped in Los Angeles International Airport in transit, one look at my swollen legs reminded me that I had a pair of expensive flight socks sitting unused in my cabin bag. Drat. I wondered how I'd forgotten to put them on until then. Better late than never, so sitting on the floor of the gate lounge, I tried to pull them on discreetly under my trousers. Yes, in hindsight I should have gone to the bathroom but I was afraid I might miss our flight call. Obviously my surreptitious fiddling under my clothing had been picked up on the CCTV camera and security had been alerted about the plump lady on the floor poking about up her trousers.

Our flight was announced. Geoffrey and I gathered our things and headed to the boarding desk where a security guard strode in front of me and asked me to step aside. I wasn't worried. I'd done nothing wrong and Geoffrey waited patiently for them to finish their 'random' check.

'What's under your trousers, ma'am?' asked the security guard.

'What?' I asked, confused. Was this a security or a pickup-line question? Perhaps he liked them plump?

'What have you got under your trousers?' he barked in a more aggressive tone.

'Umm, my legs, sir,' I replied in all honesty.

'Right, come with me. Walk through the X-ray machine.'

I did as I was asked, feeling confused about what on earth the problem was.

The X-ray was clear but a female officer then led me into a side room and explained that I'd been seen putting something under my trousers while sitting on the floor.

'Umm, ohhh, yes.' The penny dropped. 'That was my flight socks. I forgot I had them with me till I saw my swollen feet. I was worried about missing the boarding call so I put them on in the gate lounge,' I explained.

'Trousers off,' she responded.

'No, look. I'll show you,' I explained and whipped my Crocs off, noticing a look of distaste pass over her face. I rolled down the flight socks and held them up for her to inspect. Satisfied with my explanation and production of the illicit footwear, she patted my legs down before releasing me.

I returned, red-faced, to an anxious Geoffrey and we quickly scuttled on board. Once seated, I explained to him what had happened.

'You deserve to be arrested, wearing those hideous Crocs with socks,' he pointed out.

High in the sky between LA and Vancouver, Geoffrey sipped his coffee. I opened my chocolate mousse, dipped the spoon in and raised it to my mouth. That was the precise moment the universe chuckled and the plane decided to fall from the sky into a vacuum of turbulence. In the instantaneous plummet, my mousse rose up, smacked me in the face and slid down my front. Geoffrey's coffee jettisoned itself into orbit and was left dripping from the ceiling.

'Shit,' I gasped in alarm.

Shocked by the free-fall, I looked at Geoffrey in alarm. He stared back at me and laughed; chocolate mousse was plastered all over my face.

'You look like you've been dipped in a chocolate fondue,' he roared.

The cabin staff quickly moved through the aircraft, mopping up spillages and reassuring passengers. I cleaned myself up as best I could with serviettes then waited for the 'Fasten Seat Belt' sign to go off so I could head to the ladies. Finally it did so I stood up, pressing down on the headrest in front of me as I awkwardly manoeuvred myself up and out to the aisle.

'Oi, owww,' shouted a disgruntled man sitting in the seat in front of me. He twisted around angrily. Oh, my goodness. I'd missed the headrest and instead stuck my great big, mousse-smeared paw on the top of his head and inadvertently used it to spring up out of my seat. I was mortified.

'I'm so sorry. That wasn't meant to happen,' I apologised profusely and raced to the toilets. I hid in the bathroom for the amount of time I hoped it would take for someone whose head has been used as a springboard to calm down. When I returned shamefaced to my seat, I slithered in as unobtrusively as possible, keeping my hands firmly to myself.

Geoffrey glared at me and shook his head in dismay.

'It was an accident,' I whispered. 'I didn't notice his head there. I think I need a drink.'

Geoffrey just rolled his eyes and tried to read his book.

Later that night in the bathroom of our 36th floor room at the Sheraton Vancouver, I dabbed at the chocolate stains on my top before joining Geoffrey on the balcony. Below us stretched the lights of the city and boats reflecting in the calm water of the harbour. Off in the distance, Grouse Mountain skifield was lit up, shimmering brightly against the dark, mountainous backdrop. Our first impressions as we arrived earlier had been of a city wrapped around water and enclosed by snow-topped mountain peaks, with mile upon mile of green forest stretching away from the city's edge.

The next morning dawned bright and sunny and the perfume of flowering cherry blossoms followed us around Stanley Park as we strolled. In the afternoon the scent of scorched oil pervaded our nostrils and permeated the city tour bus we were taking. The vehicle shuddered and groaned; horrible graunching, gnashing sounds emitted from the engine as the young woman tried helplessly to change out of first gear.

'I'm so sorry,' called out our flustered young driver. 'It's my first day on the job.'

'Put the clutch in,' yelled someone from down the back.

'It's no use,' she shouted.

Our tour became a shortened and tortured loop of Vancouver in first gear, the engine revving loudly under the strain, only interrupted by the driver's sporadic attempts to get the bus into second gear, resulting in a return to gnashing and grinding. A queue of angry drivers formed behind us, tooting loudly. Our driver sobbed and the passengers consoled her while choking on fumes.

With our ears still ringing and our nostrils bathed in oil smoke, the time came for us to leave Vancouver. Grey skies and light drizzle greeted us as we headed towards the RV company's base in Langley aboard our new home on wheels. Geoffrey was up the front beside the driver, studying the dashboard functions. Sitting at the dining table behind them, I scanned the interior with interest.

On the open road, our speed picked up and it wasn't long before our suitcases on wheels took flight, rolling up and down the aisle. Staggering about the moving vehicle, I managed to rescue the wayward bags, securing them on the bed at the back. As I returned to my seat, I was just in time to catch our hand luggage before it slid over the edge of the dining table. Looking around for the nearest place to stow the bags, I spied the kitchen sink and the oven, ideal locations in which to immobilise moving items. Perfect. I returned to my seat.

After signing paperwork and having a demonstration of all the working parts of the campervan, we set forth, armed with maps and directions to the nearest supermarket. Geoffrey sat on the left instead of the right and drove on the right instead of the left. This would take some getting used to.

Eventually we hit the open road, heading east towards E.C. Manning Provincial Park in the Cascade Mountains. Rain drummed noisily on the aluminium roof as we drove up into thickly forested mountains. A sheer cliff on our right dropped to a fast-flowing river far below while snow-covered forest decorated the steep hill above us. Visibility was poor, the wipers struggling to clear the torrent from the windscreen. The light was fading so we decided to stop for the night and pulled into the first rest area we came to. Thunder rumbled overhead.

The place we found ourselves in was next to a swollen river and surrounded by tall Douglas fir and western red cedar trees. After a quick leg stretch in the rain, Geoffrey started to unpack, looking for our sleeping bags so that he could set up the bed. I turned the grill on to make us a quick bacon sandwich for dinner. While I was searching in the fridge for the bacon, a burning smell caught my attention. *That's weird. I haven't put anything in the oven yet. Or have I? Oh shit. Yes I have. It's Geoffrey's travel pack.* I whipped that oven door open smartly. There sat Geoffrey's pack, starting to crisp up under the grill; much longer and it would have ignited. Horrified, I yanked the van door open and chucked the bag outside onto the wet ground to cool off. Poor Geoffrey stood there looking dumbfounded.

'I forgot that was in there,' I muttered.

'I'm not even going to ask what my bag was doing in the oven,' said Geoffrey crossly.

The next morning I learnt about the quirks of a minuscule shower tub with a wrap-around curtain and a hand-held shower hose. The curtain turned itself into cling film and seemed determined to wrap me up like a sandwich. The hose on the other hand preferred its freedom, taking every opportunity to break free and drench the entire bathroom with its high-pressure nozzle. I made a mental note to use the campground showers where possible.

We drove through a valley filled with fruit orchards in blossom and vineyards in neat rows alongside Okanagan Lake then stopped at Shuswap Lake campground for the night, parking right beside the water. We spent a tranquil evening sitting by the fire watching the sun go down, sipping Kokanee Glacier Beer before being woken at 4 a.m. by geese and ducks stirring as the sun came up. A hot coffee by the lake and we were on the road again.

As we approached the Rockies, the landscape became increasingly sharp and rugged. The temperature dropped and an occasional elk crossed the Trans-Canada Highway while Roxette blared out 'Listen to Your Heart' in the background. Lake Louise lay still under layers of frozen ice in a mountain basin carved out by the Victoria Glacier. Deep snowdrifts lined the road and riverside campground, revealing some large animal footprints. That night we shivered in our sleeping bags.

After a side trip to Banff, we drove along the Icefields Parkway towards Jasper before following the snaking path of the Fraser River to Prince George. In the days that followed, we took isolated and sparsely populated roads lined with pine trees, sawmills and snow drifts, heading northwards to join the Alaska Highway at Fort St. John. The only radio station we could pick up played endless country music so John Denver kept us company on the long drive, crooning about country roads as an assortment of wildlife came in and out of view, never ceasing to enthral us.

Geoffrey drove and I cooked, an arrangement that suited us both. At the end of each day, while I got dinner ready, Geoffrey, a self-confessed pyromaniac, was happy spending his evenings stoking a fire and sampling different Canadian beers. One evening, camped beside McLeod Lake and after imbibing more than a couple of Moosehead lagers, he decided to assist me with the cooking by baking the potatoes in foil on his magnificent fire.

When dinner was ready, I handed Geoffrey a picnic plate for the potatoes. He proudly unwrapped the foil and tipped his spuds onto it. They fell with a thump. There sat what looked like four smoking meteorites, still hot from a burning entry into our atmosphere. We stared; the picnic plate withered.

'You did that on purpose, didn't you?' I accused. 'It's payback for me cooking your bag.'

But Geoffrey blamed the fire, and the strong Moosehead lager.

We sat companionably by the fire's embers, watching the sun set in a yellow blaze behind the mountains. We could hear an occasional splash as fish disturbed the lake's surface. Squirrels rustled around, delighting us with their antics, scurrying up and down the trees, and a marmot popped its head up from the ground nearby, looking at us quizzically before bobbing down again. The scent of wood smoke filled the air, deterring the hovering, ever-present mosquitoes. As the sun dipped, the air grew chilly and the first stars slowly appeared.

Later, homeward bound, we sat in the food court area at Vancouver International Airport, waiting to catch a Canadian Airlines flight back to Australia. Looking around the café, I announced, 'Look, that man's got exactly the same bag as ours.' Geoffrey went to turn around to see but I quickly interjected with, 'No, don't look now. He's looking.' The man turned away again. 'Quick, look now,' I blurted. Geoffrey swivelled around and stared.

'It's a flipping mirror,' he groaned, glaring at me. 'Of course it's the same bag; it's ours. And make sure you put your flight socks on before we get to the gate. I don't want another fiasco,' he warned.

'Don't worry. I'm not going to attract any sort of trouble today,' I announced confidently.

High over the North Pacific Ocean, the gentleman in the seat next to me started to vomit blood. I pressed the panic button. The crew panicked. I panicked some more and an urgent call went out for a doctor. The gentleman was swiftly carted up to the front of the aircraft to receive medical treatment. Geoffrey woke up to what looked like a crime scene and a hostess mopping up blood. Wide-eyed he stared at me accusingly.

'What?' I asked.

1996

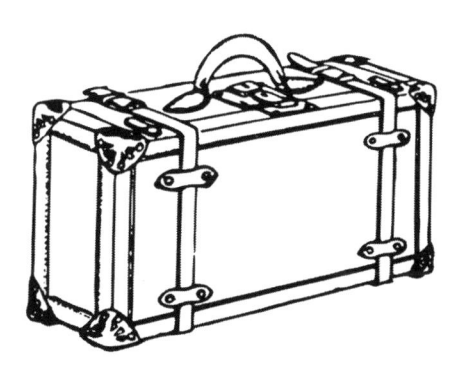

USA

THOMAS TOURS THE STATES

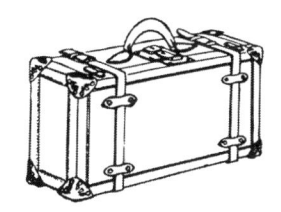

Geoffrey and I farewelled Melbourne and returned to jobs in Wellington in 1992. We bought a house on the Kapiti Coast before our first child, Jan, arrived the following year. This kept us happily grounded for the next few years, busy with a growing toddler.

Our next big adventure was a long-anticipated return to Vancouver in 1996, only this time there was a difference—there were now three of us, and one of us was literally three. We were now attempting international travel as a trio, with our daughter Jan in tow. She'd celebrated her third birthday two days before departure with a party featuring trains and Barney the dinosaur, a hint at things to come on this trip.

'So who is this Thomas from the chapter title?' you ask. Well, Thomas the Tank Engine came with us too, and not only Thomas but all his friends. Geoffrey, Jan and I travelled economy. Thomas and his friends travelled first class in a specially designed, limited-edition carrying case shaped like Thomas the Tank Engine. With Thomas along for the ride, I guess that made me the Fat Controller.

From a starting point in Vancouver, we planned a one-month route through the Canadian Rockies then south through Montana and Wyoming. Heading west we would then travel across Idaho and Oregon to the Oregon Coast before pointing north up through Washington, returning to Vancouver. We were once again travelling in a seven-metre RV. Having a home on wheels meant Jan could sleep in the same bed every night, providing familiarity. Plus we had the added convenience of not having to pack and unpack continually. The theme for the trip was set—trains, dinosaurs, Geoffrey's fires, wildlife spotting and spectacular scenery.

Jan's bed was a bunk above the driving cab. She thought this was ever so exciting. She had all her toys and sleeping bag up there along with a collection of favourite books she brought from home. The most popular at the time was *I Love Animals* by Flora McDonnell. With a Scottish-sounding name like that, we couldn't resist reading the book in an extremely exaggerated Scottish burr. This sent not only Jan, but all of us, into fits of giggles. The nightly routine before bed was Scottish time with Flora and a whole lot of laughing. All that could be heard from within our van was 'och aye the nooo' and hysterical laughter.

We had the freedom to stop for the night at will, wherever or whenever we wanted—a bonus with a toddler in tow. There was certainly no shortage of picturesque lakeside campgrounds surrounded by forests of green lodgepole pine. The sites were usually equipped with picnic tables, a campfire and wood. Geoffrey typically started his fire while I got dinner on. This time instead of chicken casserole fit for a coyote, which Geoffrey and I had tried to tuck into with disastrous consequences the last time we'd been in Canada, chicken nuggets fit for a three-year-old were heavily featured on the menu. Jan would set up her Thomas trains all over the picnic table, and instead of a table dedicated to Canadian beers, as in that previous trip, it was now shared with those pesky trains.

In between stoking his fire and sipping a beer, Geoffrey feigned interest in each train that Jan presented for inspection. Thomas and accomplices were lined up in order of preference to be examined one by one. Alternatively the tracks would be set up going around the picnic table for the trains to weave their way past cans of Canadian lager. On one occasion, while Geoffrey was dutifully surveying the ever-present trains, we heard a loud toot. A real, live, shiny black steam engine chugged past in the distance, steam billowing and horn tooting. Jan jumped up and down in excitement.

'Train, train,' she shouted.

'Let's hope it's a long one,' muttered Geoffrey, enjoying a break from the never-ending train talk.

Dinner outside by the crackling fire was usually followed by a stroll through the pine-scented forest at toddler speed, pausing to gaze with interest at squirrels. If we were at a lake, we'd select perfect skimming stones from the shore for bouncing across the glassy lake surface.

The tedious trainspotting continued in Jasper. Canada, it appeared, was filled with trains; there was no escape. We soaked up about as much train-themed knowledge as anyone could possibly endure, with just the right amount of parental enthusiasm on display.

Driving through the Rockies, Geoffrey suddenly hit the brakes and swerved to a stop at the side of the road. Leaping from his seat, he then flew out of the van door, shouting, 'Bears.'

Grabbing Jan, I quickly joined Geoffrey outside, where we stood watching from a distance as a mother black bear and her two cubs browsed the vegetation beside the highway, looking for berries. We stayed right beside the van, quietly observing in awe as they calmly ignored us, grazed then moved further into the thicket out of sight. I shivered. It was freezing out.

Further on, driving through a craggy mountain pass, we were delighted with the first snowfall of autumn. Crystalline drifts formed at the corners of our windscreen as the temperature plummeted at such high altitude. The pine trees were soon dusted in a coating of powdery-white snow. As soon as we could, we pulled off the road to park before dashing out into the wintery wonderland to play, firing snowballs at one another and making a handsome-looking snowman.

'What shall we call your snowman?' I asked Jan.

'Thomas,' she replied.

I noticed Geoffrey roll his eyes.

Later that evening, Jan climbed up to her bunk and before long reappeared proffering a Thomas book titled *Thomas & Friends: The Great Snow Storm of Sodor*. We stared at it with a smiley grimace.

'Wish he'd sod off,' whispered Geoffrey.

But did I mention dinosaurs? Well, thankfully there were no Barney theme parks near Vancouver but there was a seriously close and just as naff second—Dinotown at Bridal Falls, a world of big, brightly coloured dinosaurs based on Bedrock City from the Flintstones. The place was perfect for a child but not so much for Geoffrey. The Flintstones' theme music blasting out of speakers on repeat and overly cheery park attendants grated on his nerves.

Jan's attention was drawn to a Flintstones' pedal car. She insisted on sitting up front next to Geoffrey and as she couldn't reach the pedals, he was left to do all the work while the Fat Controller lounged in the back. The result was remarkably similar to the TV show where Fred's and Barney's feet pedal at the speed of light to propel the car. So who could blame me for launching into a few lines set to the theme tune?

> 'Let's drive with the Hayhursts in the heat
> Through the pedalling of Geoffrey's giant feet,
> When you're in the back seat
> Have a yabba-dabba-doo time
> A dabba-doo time
> Jan's having a great old time…'

From the comfort of the back seat, I laughed out loud at my joke while Geoffrey sweated buckets turning those pedals. Jan sat next to him, grinning from ear to ear at this splendid activity. As we slowly did a lap of the park, Geoffrey's face turned an alarming shade of scarlet. At the end, an exhausted Geoffrey staggered out, legs like jelly.

'Come on, Daddy, hurry,' called Jan, grabbing his sweaty hand. A crowd was forming.

It was the Dino street parade leading to the dinosaur stage for Dee Dee's dinosaur sing-a-long. Strutting, clappy-clappy T-Rexes actively promoted audience participation. Jan danced and sang with animated enthusiasm. I did my best to clap and sing along. Geoffrey looked pained.

As we moved south, leaving the chilly mountains behind, we marvelled at the endless blue Montana skies above vast plains of waving gold crops. Searing heat wrapped itself around us, while Jan wrapped herself proudly in her new Dinotown T-shirt. Geoffrey grimaced every time he looked at it; his legs were still sore. Our RV bumped over dusty gravel roads onto the Flathead Indian Reservation lands where we drove through the National Bison Range, hopeful of seeing some animals wandering in the distance. As we rounded a corner, an entire herd of magnificent bison were strolling all over the road; some lay snoozing while others casually chewed at the tough, yellow grass.

We stopped in our tracks as the herd turned and eyed us with disdain. The enormous male among them ambled towards our RV. He just kept coming, heavily plodding. Eyeballing us, the bison approached the van until he was at touching distance. Our eyes widened. I held my breath. He came to my door; he was massive. I froze. He stared menacingly at us then nonchalantly rubbed and scratched his head against my wing mirror, keeping one beady brown eye on us. Dust and tufts of bison hair came adrift. His breath steamed up the window.

'Big coos,' called out Jan, making me jump.

Oh no. She's talking Scottish now from that damn book. 'Cows,' I corrected. 'No, no, I mean bison. Bison, not cows.'

We were enthralled to see bison in the wild and so close we could have scratched behind their ears by winding down the window. We could certainly smell them. Our brochure warned that we could be gored to death by one as they can weigh as much as 900 kilos and sprint at 50 kilometres per hour. 'Stay in your vehicle at all times,' it said. No argument from us there.

We couldn't resist a nearby detour to see a ghost town. Garnet Ghost Town was reached via a narrow, unpaved road winding through the forest. After parking, we followed a dirt track on foot through the trees. The ghost town revealed itself, nestled in a cleared meadow carpeted with wild flowers. There was a hushed stillness about the place; even the birds had fallen silent. We were the only living souls there, with a noticeable absence of squirrels or other wildlife.

A sign at the entrance explained a little of the history. Garnet Ghost Town had come into existence in the 1890s because of gold found in the quartz-rich ground a few decades earlier. Miners had established a bustling wee town boasting hotels, saloons, stores, a school and a barbershop, but by 1920 the place was abandoned. It now stood deserted and silent.

When we peered into the tumbledown buildings, it felt as if you could reach out and touch the past, a place where history could be absorbed while walking the floorboards. We gingerly stepped inside the dance hall, saloon and school room. They were fascinating but eerily quiet; it seemed like the past wanted to be left alone so we bade farewell.

That night, Jan worryingly disappeared up to her bunk again. Geoffrey looked at me.

'There's surely not a Thomas book about a ghost town?' He sighed.

'Can't be,' I replied.

'Who bought her those damn books anyway?'

We shushed as Jan clambered down the ladder clutching a book in her hand. She hopped up at the table and presented it to Geoffrey. The title read *Thomas & Friends: The Ghost Engine*. I glanced at Geoffrey with raised eyebrows but made no comment.

Our campervan entered Wyoming through the immense 9,000-square-kilometre Yellowstone National Park wilderness area. Yellowstone is known for its waterfalls, rivers, canyons, geysers and thermal features. Animal species include bears, wolves, bison, elk and antelope. Jan took in the sights enthusiastically, watching mud pools glug and gurgle and waiting with anticipation for Old Faithful the geyser to erupt. As we toured the park, camping and exploring, it felt as if we were in an untouched paradise. Waking up to find our campervan surrounded by grazing elk was just the icing on the cake.

As we headed south, the slopes of the Grand Teton Mountain Range in Wyoming were bathed in the golden foliage of aspens. Autumn was here, contradicted by the baking hot sun we were experiencing. Jan continued to wear her Dinotown T-shirt. Geoffrey's leg muscles slowly recovered.

A massive storm was brewing as we crossed into Idaho. The sky grew darker, blotting out the sun so we decided to stop before it hit. Thunder rumbled in the distance and lightning flashes lit up the dark clouds. The sky looked menacing. We stopped at Snake River Falls, alone in a large, deserted camp ground, then headed out into the forest for a quick walk to stretch our legs, our feet scuffing up fallen leaves and pine needles as fat raindrops arrived, sending us scuttling back to the RV.

We ate dinner inside that night as the storm raged, the rain loud against the aluminium roof. I locked the door; with no other campers about, we felt a little isolated. Jan had a captive audience so out came that damn Thomas collection. And out came a Canadian beer. Thomas and his mates scuttled around the dining table and soon we were ready for Scottish time with Flora McDonnell. Geoffrey tucked himself up onto the top bunk with Jan to read it in his Scottish voice.

'One more story, Daddy,' begged Jan and, quick as a flash, presented Geoffrey with *Thomas & Friends: Thomas and the Terrible Storm*.

Once Jan was asleep, Geoffrey whispered to me, 'Is there nothing that f#@%ing train hasn't done?'

The next day the weather had cleared. The previous night's rain was fast evaporating in rising layers of steaming mist under a warm sun, leaving the forest floor damp and richly scented. We set off through Craters of the Moon National Monument & Preserve, along the Snake River Plain in Central Idaho. The preservation area covers over 1,600 kilometres, encompassing three major lava fields formed by volcanic eruptions that started 15,000 years ago. The lumpy black ocean of lava and sagebrush steppe were broken up by occasional buttes rising from the flat horizon.

We stopped to view Big Butte. Yes, I'm serious. They are rhyolitic volcanic domes. Big Butte, as its name would suggest, is one of the largest volcanic domes in the world at 2,300 metres. We'd never heard of these geological features before. I had to admire the person who had dared to name one Big Butte. Of course a photo opportunity was called for.

Travelling onwards and heading west, we followed in the footsteps of the early pioneers along the Oregon Trail, across plains filled with wild sunflowers. Centuries-old wagon-wheel ruts crisscross the dry, dusty earth, forever imprinted upon the ground. The sight of these ruts completely floored me; living history that told a story like no book could ever capture. A visit to the Oregon Trail visitor centre was a fascinating step back in time; a rich history lesson told through actors, artefacts, photos, film, diary entries and recreated wagon life scenes. This was an incredible experience.

We stopped to explore the painted mountains in central Oregon at the John Day Fossil Beds National Monument. Fossils of numerous ancient mammal and plant species have been preserved here by volcanic eruptions. As we walked, the sun radiated off the arid, rocky landscape, picking out the layered colours of ochre, rust, red, orange and yellow laid down over many years of volcanic activity. Everything was silent other than the crunch of volcanic debris under our feet, a landscape just begging for a child's imagination to conjure up roaming dinosaurs.

'You don't think Thomas has a book about volcanos or dinosaurs, do you?' whispered Geoffrey, looking worried.

'No, I doubt it. The Island of Sodor has sod all on it as far as I can see from the books. We should be safe,' I foolishly replied.

As we walked towards the west, we could see another storm brewing in the direction we were headed. The sky was turning an angry purple.

We set off in the RV to cross over the 1,800-metre McKenzie Pass to the Oregon Coast. At the top, we found ourselves caught in a blizzard. Driving sleet and hail lashed the windscreen, reducing visibility and forcing us to pull off the road a few times. We shivered as the temperature plummeted, grabbing extra clothes to put on and covering Jan who slept through it all in her car seat. Slushy snow lay in pockets across the road, making driving conditions hazardous and progress slow. The cab was silent as Geoffrey concentrated, gripping the steering wheel tightly. We were relieved to make it safely down the other side of the pass to the lush green and wet Oregon Coast.

That night we camped snuggled down in the lee of the sand dunes next to a roaring surf beach. Jan climbed the ladder to fossick about in her box of books. Geoffrey and I looked at each other with raised eyebrows. *Surely not. There's no way.* Jan climbed down the ladder and slapped a book on the table. *Thomas & Friends: Thomas and the Volcano* read the title. 'Oh, and what was the description?' you might wonder. *Thomas and his friends see a volcano in the new Dinosaur Park.* Geoffrey and I looked at each other across Jan's head, eyes rolled and Geoffrey mouthed something rude.

Our travel along the wild, wet and wind-swept Oregon Coast was peppered with seal watching, beachcombing, lighthouses and shipwrecks. Tumultuous surf thundered the west-coast beaches, rolling in with unpredictable force, threatening to sweep us off our feet. Jan giggled as we repeatedly grabbed her and ran, laughing as we dashed, our hair adrift, faces lashed in salt spray. Oh, the power of that surf. With the ever-present Pacific Ocean on our left, we needed to head north through Seattle on the final leg of our travels back to Vancouver, homeward bound.

I later reflected on the differences between our first trip to Canada as a couple and this trip, our first with a child.

The first trip was Roxette music, relaxing, chicken casserole, reading novels and singing along to Bob Seger. Travelling with Jan, it was Barney the dinosaur music, lessons on trains, chicken nuggets, Thomas books and singing with naff Dinoland dinosaurs. There wasn't that much difference between the two trips, was there? Taking journeys with a small child just required a healthy dose of patience and a tolerance towards train buffs.

Note: Jan didn't grow up to become a train driver or even a trainspotter. Thankfully she went off trains soon afterwards and that pesky Thomas went back into his carrying case. But I couldn't part with dear Thomas. Even though Jan left home long ago, he and his companions still sit on a shelf in her bedroom. However, the Thomas books seemed to go missing not long after we returned. I suspect Geoffrey had something to do with that.

2004

WEST COAST, NEW ZEALAND

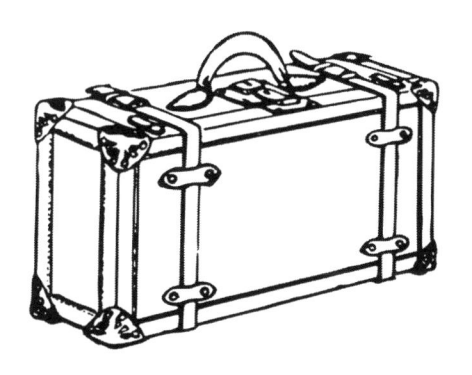

IT WAS HIM. HE DID IT!

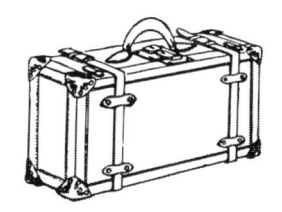

The trip to Canada and the USA with Jan had been our last overseas travel for a few years while we raised our family. Jan had been joined by a younger brother, Don, in 2000, and let's just say he wasn't the sort of youngster you would take on a long plane ride. He was a typically loud and active boy, and I should know, as I was his teacher. His pre-school had hired me as lunchtime cover, which eventually progressed to full-time teaching.

In the summer of 2004, we visited our family at Motunau Beach then drove over to the West Coast of the South Island to stay in a small seaside village called Punakaiki. The spectacular drive showcased bush-clad coast plunging directly from the mountains of the Paparoa National Park into the Tasman Sea. We arrived at a new holiday accommodation complex built just above the Punakaiki River, a short walk from Pancake Rocks and Blowholes. The apartments sat among lush, native rainforest filled with New Zealand nīkau palms and silver ferns.

We settled in and unpacked. Geoffrey and I made a coffee and sat down to recover from the long, tiring drive while the kids were mucking around playing in the bedroom. Jan was sporting a huge black eye which she was still angry at me about. What? No, I didn't hit her. Don did.

Let me explain. Back at home I'd been on the phone a couple of days prior, having a nice chat with a friend. Ten-year-old Jan interrupted to tell me Don had hit her. Now, Don was only four and not very big. How much harm could he have done to a ten-year-old? So I waved her away, despite her insisting he'd really hurt her. *Sibling squabbles. They'll make amends.*

By the time I finished my conversation and inspected the damage, Jan had the makings of a black eye appearing. It developed further overnight into its full, technicolour glory. By the next morning, Jan was sporting a vivid red, purple and black eye just in time to go on holiday. I peered closely at it, my face giving away a look of distaste at the dreadfully discoloured, puffy tissue. Jan was still miffed at me for ignoring her at the time of the incident. I felt guilty. I never did get to the bottom of why Don had socked her one. Perhaps it was accidental or perhaps not.

Anyway, coffees in hand, Geoffrey and I relaxed, taking in the beauty of the surroundings. Suddenly, a piercing scream echoed loudly around the apartment, the sort of scream that indicated something serious. Rushing into the bedroom, we found Don sobbing and holding his forehead. Jan was standing next to him. *Has she sought sweet revenge?*

In between Don's sobs, Jan explained what had happened while I pressed a cold cloth to his head. Don had been having a merry old time bouncing from our bed mattress across to his trundler bed. He'd mistimed his jump, slipped between the two beds and smashed his forehead on the metal bed frame. His head wasn't just bruised. It had a lump, a big lump. I hurriedly wrapped ice cubes inside the cold cloth.

Once Don was calm again and the cold compress had been on the lump for a good ten minutes, we had another look. The lump was growing and was now protruding out of his forehead like a giant egg. It looked like his forehead was the receptacle for incubating an emu egg. We needed to seek medical advice in case of concussion. So, coffees abandoned, we all bundled back into the car again and drove to the nearest doctor's surgery in Greymouth, a small coastal town. Upon arrival we were asked to have a seat in the waiting room after the receptionist took some details.

There we sat in the doctor's surgery, strangers in town, one child with a mighty black eye and the second with a massive head trauma. *Well, this isn't one bit awkward*, I thought, looking around me at the other patients furtively glancing our way. A nurse walked in and the receptionist whispered something to her before looking in our direction. The nurse glanced across at us over the top of her glasses, frowning ever so slightly, her lips forming a hard line. I gulped.

The nurse showed us into the doctor's office and passed him a piece of paper with a note on it. *I bet I know what that says*: *Psssttt, don't look now, but I think these two are child abusers*. The doctor looked across at Jan, studying her intently with a furrowed brow, and asked her what had happened to her eye. Geoffrey interrupted to tell him *she* wasn't the patient; we were here about Don. But the doctor shushed him and looked directly at Jan.

'You can tell me the truth,' he said. 'Did somebody do this to you?'

'Yes,' she said emphatically.

'It wasn't an accident, was it?' he asked.

'No, it was not,' she stated a tad too firmly.

'He did it,' she said, pointing an accusatory finger at Don, 'and Mum didn't even care,' she continued.

Oh, flipping heck. I groaned inwardly. *Not this again. Make her stop*. I cringed in shame.

'Who did it?' snapped the doctor. 'Your father or your mother?'

'Now hang on a minute,' said Geoffrey, getting highly irritated.

'What?' asked Jan. 'No. Him. Don, my stupid brother.'

'How could he do this to you? He's only little. That would require quite some force,' interjected Mr know-it-all doctor.

'I know. It really, really hurt and Mum wouldn't even help me,' Jan replied, enjoying her moment in the spotlight. I glared at her across the room.

'This is ridiculous,' I snapped. 'Can you look at Don's head please? He's the patient.'

'I have a duty of care,' he replied, 'to ensure children are not being harmed.'

I'll bloody harm you in a minute. The cheek.

The doctor turned to Don and asked, 'And how did this happen, young man?'

Don was shy and just hugged his crocodile, Gary, without replying.

Geoffrey responded for him and explained what had happened, adding, 'Jan was with him at the time. Ask her. Seems you clearly don't believe us.'

'Is this true?' the doctor asked Jan.

'Yep, it is. He was bouncing around being Tigger the tiger and fell on his dumb head but that will teach him for punching me,' she replied.

'Right, I guess that clears that up then,' said the doctor and finally got on with examining Don's egg head, without apology.

Once this was done and Don was pronounced OK, we shuffled shamefaced, feeling humiliated, out to reception where everyone could see the poor battered children. We paid the account while being glared at by the frosty-faced receptionist before slinking out, red-faced.

Geoffrey got in the car and slammed the door. We drove back to the cottage in silence. *Well, that was a great start to the holiday.*

Our reputation as visiting child abusers was cemented later that night as screams of terror rang out from our cottage and around the holiday village. The sounds of a child in terrible distress could be heard emanating from within our walls. What was happening?

Don was having his first-ever shower and a drop of water had touched his face.

He'd only ever had baths at home where it was easy to keep water off his face, but the cottage only had a shower. He loved water, but not on his face or in his eyes. So Don would be remaining unwashed for the rest of the stay apparently. Not to worry, the next day would be better.

A bright and sunny day greeted us with a morning chorus of birds from the surrounding native bush. The cicadas started their raspy chirping as we set off down the track to the Punakaiki river mouth below us, picnic bags in hand. Geoffrey and I had an ulterior motive— get Don in the river for at least a bit of a wash. As we reached the gravelly river bed and picked our way over the rocks towards the water's edge, something was amiss. Each crunching step dislodged a cloud of black sandflies, the West Coast's bloodsucking summer nightmare.

'Don't worry. They'll leave us alone in a minute. We've just disturbed them,' I said, theorising. 'Let's just go straight in the water for a paddle.'

Clouds of beasties swirled around us. We kept moving in the river to deter them. A while later I tentatively left the safety of the water to set up the picnic blanket and food. Geoffrey, Jan and Don clambered back over the slippery stones to wrap themselves in towels.

Hungry humans tried to eat. Hungry sandflies began eating their prey, tearing at skin using saw-like barbs to widen tiny wounds and suck out blood. Once again screams rang out around the bay. Hands slapped. The sandflies intensified their attack, honing in on arms, necks, faces and feet, multiple bites rendering the receivers with nasty swelling, itching hives and a general desire to scream.

Food was flung. Bags were grabbed. Bodies scampered across the gravel, up the track, over the road and into our unit. The door was slammed, tears were dried and wounds were bathed. When we next stepped outdoors, we looked like we all had a good dose of the pox, covered as we were head to toe in splodges of chalky-white calamine lotion liberally dotting our swollen bites. We spent the rest of the week demented with itching and scratching. Night-time was the worst, squirming beneath the sheets, all hot and hivey.

As a family we decided we preferred a holiday destination where you could sit outside without having your blood sucked out of your body. We never returned.

2006

FRANCE AND ITALY

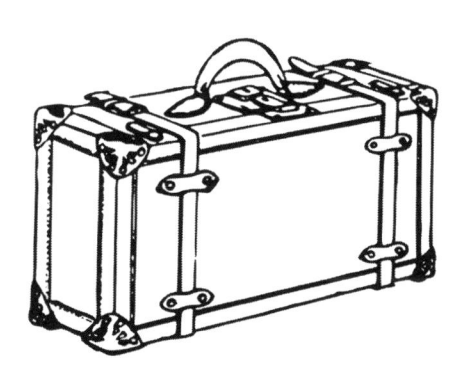

THE CATAPULT

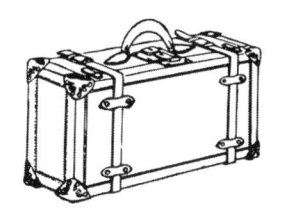

Two years after our disastrous West Coast holiday, Don was now six and almost tamed apart from his fascination with weaponry. And a big plus—water was allowed to touch his face. We were ready to attempt international travel as a foursome. So after much scrimping and saving, sweet-talking the bank and our accommodating employers, we set out to see a bit of the world.

In the autumn of 2006, we set off on our first-ever adventure exploring Europe by car. In hindsight we tried to cram too much into our three months away, resulting in long hours sitting in a car and not enough time to explore each place fully. But it gave us a taster of places we wanted to return to and a lesson for future trips.

We were now exhausted after travelling for eight weeks, during which we'd flown into Heathrow and then driven around the UK in a rental car, spending a week in Cornwall visiting relatives before making our way up to Plockton in Scotland. After doing a small loop of the country, we'd caught the ferry over to Belfast to visit my family before driving a hurried circuit around Ireland. We'd taken a ferry back to the UK and driven across to Dover before catching the ferry to Calais.

So it was with a sense of relief that we arrived in the pretty French hilltop village of Bonnieux, located in the Luberon region of Provence. We were there for a week and breathed a sigh of relief that we could stay put for more than a night or two.

Our accommodation was an apartment at The Old Gendarmerie, an amazing conversion of the original police building, with a rich history of accommodating officers of French law. With its three levels of sashed windows framed by pale-blue shutters, this solid, terracotta-rendered building stood facing onto the heart of the village. Within, its thick walls, high ceilings and exposed beams led the eye up a worn staircase fitted with a decorative wrought-iron railing. Inside the apartment, terracotta-tiled floors complemented the original whitewashed beams and exposed stone walls.

We noticed Bonnieux had a village hairdresser. After two months of travelling, our hair had grown long and straggly and we were beginning to resemble wild-haired puppets from *The Muppet Show*; something would have to be done. Our French was limited to standard tourist phrases and the French travel guide completely lacked any useful words for communicating with a French-speaking hairdresser. One morning we noticed the salon was open, so we crossed our fingers and timidly entered, hoping to muster enough French to make an appointment.

'*Bonjour, madame, parlez-vous anglais?*' I ventured.

'*Non, madame, désolé*,' she replied.

I looked at Geoffrey in desperation. He sighed and shrugged. It was up to me. Inspiration hit me. I grabbed Don and pulled him forward, using my fingers to mime out snip, snip, snipping through his hair.

'Ahhh, *oui*, come, come,' called madame.

'What, right now?' I asked, surprised.

But madame wasn't listening. Don was passed along to the capable hands of her assistant.

Next I reached up, took hold of Geoffrey's head to use as a prop and did more Marcel Marceau miming with vigorous chopping motions on his scalp. I tried to convey a trim for Jan and me by showing about half an inch between my fingers. Jan was sent to wait for Don to finish and madame got busy with my hair. She expertly and neatly chopped it into the shape of a pudding bowl, which she may have loosely termed a French bob. Mushroom cap on a neck would have been my description. I grimaced with every snip until finally the ordeal was over and she proudly revealed my new look in the mirror. I looked like a man.

Madame took my nonplussed expression for a sign of approval and smiled in delight at her creation. Geoffrey's turn. I hopped down to wait. Don came to sit with me. He now looked like he was ready to serve in the French military. *Oh flip. If they ruin Jan's hair, we'll never hear the end of it!*

'Mum, she cut all my hair off.' Don groaned. The only positive I could think of was that he would be cooler in the heat. He sat staring at the floor looking glum and I mourned the accumulated pile of his blonde locks lying on the floor.

The buzz of clippers caught my attention. Geoffrey's eyes bored into mine, reflected in the mirror. He was also being scalped, seemingly ready to enter the French military academy alongside Don. *Oh Lord, what if they cut Jan's hair into a mushroom like mine?* Jan was looking alarmed as the girl snipped away merrily. Thankfully the hairdresser had produced a book of hairstyles and Jan was able to point to something less horrid than what had befallen our quiffs. Why had I not been shown some pictures instead of being turned into a walking fungus head? Jan caught my attention.

'Mum, you have to make her stop. Quick. It's getting too short. How do you say stop in French?'

I looked at Geoffrey. Again, more shrugging, sigh. I desperately searched inside the vacant doors of my brain then took a stab in the dark.

'Enough, stop, *non, non* more,' I called out. The girl continued snipping merrily.

'Do something, Mum,' cried Jan, near to tears by now as her hair fluttered to the floor.

I leapt up and made the universal sign of cut. But it was unintentionally more like 'off with your head' as I whipped a threatening, finger-pointing hand across the front of my neck. The young woman paused, looking at me with alarm. *Oh shit. Have I just threatened to behead her? What if she calls the* gendarmes? As an afterthought, I shouted a little too loudly, 'Finito, arrest, cease and desist,' just digging myself further into a hole as I panicked and blurted whatever came into my head. Denise strikes again.

The hairdresser stared at me with astonishment, scissors paused mid-air. Madame said something to the girl and she hurriedly removed Jan's cape, giving me furtive looks. Geoffrey quickly paid and we shuffled shamefaced out of the shop. Two French lieutenants emerged, one tall, one short, followed by a sculptured fungus and a chic French mademoiselle. The kids looked traumatised. It was time to visit the Bonnieux boulangerie; four lemon tarts should restore our equilibrium. And perhaps a baguette wouldn't go amiss.

As we returned to The Old Gendarmerie, I commented that it was fitting that Geoffrey and Don now had French lieutenant haircuts to go with our French officers of the law accommodation.

During our week at Bonnieux, we had a day trip to visit Château des Baux, a fortified castle built during the 10th century and located in Les Baux-de-Provence. The Lords of Baux ruled the fortress and the small town it protects for 500 years during a time of much conflict around Provence. There we got to see the biggest trebuchet in Europe, a type of catapult that uses a long arm to throw a projectile. Naturally anything involving weaponry was bound to attract Don's attention. The requisite exit via the gift shop resulted in the purchase of a mini working model of a catapult to accompany a book containing magical illustrations of castles, forts, knights and armour. We were by now sporting an ever-growing collection of model knights on horseback.

When we got back to our apartment, Geoffrey sat in the lounge to read; Jan went to her room to relax and Don sat on the lounge floor surrounded by his assortment of knights and the brand-new trebuchet which he sat playing with while I prepared dinner in the open-plan kitchen. Without warning, there was a loud cracking sound as Don's catapult was found to be in stellar working order when it efficiently fired a ball bearing at the speed of light directly into the glass sliding door.

'Shit,' said Geoffrey, dropping his book in fright and leaping to his feet.

Jan dashed out of the bedroom to see what had happened and looked around.

Don sat on the floor and announced, 'Wow, cool,' and went to locate the ball bearing.

'Oh no, you don't,' I said. 'You nearly smashed the glass door. Just fire it gently towards the couch cushions or the catapult is getting confiscated.'

Exploring the upper reaches of Bonnieux village on foot during the week, we reached the 86 steps leading to the 12th-century Catholic high church, or *église haute*, at the highest point of the village. We climbed the steps, puffing and panting in the heat, eager to explore and gain views across the Luberon Valley from the vantage point at the top. On the way up, we paused many times while Jan patted and befriended the semi-wild cat population of Bonnieux.

When we reached the top, we opened the big, heavy church doors to look inside. They creaked, groaning loudly as we pushed them open. Inside the gloomy interior, we were surprised to find a gentleman solemnly instructing a hushed group in the art of bell ringing. All eyes turned towards us. We paused, realising we were interrupting. The bell-ringer frowned over the top of his glasses.

'Oh sorry,' I muttered, reversing out. But before I had a chance to close the cumbersome doors, Geoffrey skidded in his sandals on the slippery slate. He lost his footing and careered out of control, stumbling down the church steps and emitting an embarrassing faux pas by shouting, 'Jesus.'

Mortified I turned back to close the church doors. I expected a sea of disapproving faces but I noticed the bell-ringer was not so subtly trying to control his mirth at our uncouth intrusion.

'So sorry,' I mumbled again before pressing the heavy doors closed.

Jan was bent over, slapping at her legs. 'I've got fleas,' she exclaimed, staring in horror at her legs.

'Cool,' said Don.

'I told you not to touch those cats,' I scolded.

We headed back to our top-floor apartment at The Old Gendarmerie. Jan went to get some itchy-bite cream for her legs while Don sat down on the floor to play with his Les Baux catapult. I reminded him again that he wasn't to fire the large metal ball bearing towards the glass sliding door. A few minutes later, I looked up from where I was preparing lunch, just in time to see Don take aim and fire the catapult with all the force he could muster. The metal ball bearing shot out of the catapult at the speed of light, firing through the air, across the apartment and straight out through the sliding door. We heard a loud smash from somewhere below.

'Don,' we all shouted in unison.

He jumped, looking surprised at our reaction. 'But I didn't aim at the glass door. It was open,' he wailed indignantly.

We all rushed out to the balcony. One of the terracotta roof tiles of the apartment below had been sheared in two.

I told Don off. Geoffrey went downstairs to let the owners know and Don sulked because his precious catapult had been confiscated.

The weather was sweltering so after our lunch of French baguette, cherries and peaches, Geoffrey and Don headed to an outdoor swimming pool at Saint-Saturnin-lès-Apt which was a bit more child-friendly than our apartment's deep and icily cold one. Jan and I opted to stay behind. Later we planned to browse the wee boutiques around

Bonnieux. The boys changed into their board shorts and headed off to the swimming pool.

They returned not that much later, still bone dry, hot and grumbly. Don stomped into the bedroom and threw himself on the bed.

'Was the pool closed?' I asked.

'No, they wouldn't let us in,' said Geoffrey.

'What d'you mean? What on earth did you two do to get yourselves banned from a pool?'

'We didn't have undies on,' called Don from the bedroom.

Jan guffawed and we looked at each other more confused than ever.

'What are you talking about?' I asked.

'We weren't wearing ball warmers,' grimaced Geoffrey.

'Daaad,' said Jan, horrified. 'Ewww.'

'Sluggos, budgie smugglers, ball huggers,' he said, on a roll now and a bit grumpy.

'That's ridiculous. You were both wearing perfectly good board shorts made for swimming in,' I said, astounded.

'What archaic rules, utter nonsense,' muttered Geoffrey.

'Oh well, you'll just have to take Don down to our pool and hold onto him, even though the water's freezing.'

Don came out of his room.

'Or I could practise firing the catapult from the balcony into the pool?' he suggested with a cheeky grin.

EXCUSE ME, SIR. THERE'S AN OLIVE ON YOUR HEAD

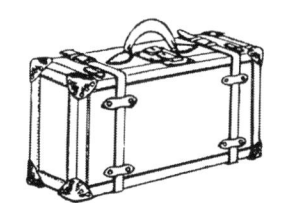

From Bonnieux, our little posse of Kiwis continued on to Lake Como in Italy, our first-ever foray onto Italian soil and an introduction to the Italian way of life and cultural differences. Our arrival at Lake Como was an unforgettable experience which some of you will have read about in *Travels with Geoffrey*. In summary, we lost Lake Como and accidentally found Switzerland instead. Don spotted a salamander; Geoffrey just about had a seizure and our accommodation was perched on top of a mountain.

After leaving Lake Como, we were going to spend our second week in Italy at Villa Orlandino near Sant'Agata sui Due Golfi on the Sorrentine Peninsula. Our much-desired destination was the Amalfi Coast, a 50-kilometre stretch of coastline along the southern edge of the peninsula. The road is set high upon sheer cliffs winding between pastel-coloured fishing villages, grand villas, terraced vineyards and cliffside lemon groves, making it a popular holiday destination. Positano is the Amalfi Coast's crowning jewel. However, we didn't have jewel-encrusted wallets. Hence we would be staying in a small, semi-rural spot at the top of the headland. Sant'Agata is surrounded by cultivated terraces of olives and views out to the Tyrrhenian Sea and the Gallos Islands.

En route we successfully managed to skirt Naples. It wasn't until leaving the *autostrada* (motorway) and encountering our first intersection at the town of Castellammare di Stabia that we ran into difficulty. A scene of madness confronted us. The Italian drivers appeared to be stark raving bonkers, clearly not culturally inclined to follow rules. Before us, we had a large, multi-exit intersection to get across, with traffic lights in perfect working order. The other drivers studiously ignored the lights as though they didn't exist. Geoffrey paused, staring wide-eyed at the melee before us, wondering what to do.

There didn't appear to be a normal, law-abiding way to get across. Everyone was just doing whatever the heck they wanted: scooters, Vespas (with helmetless riders), three-wheeled Piaggio Apes and cars, all driving directly at each other from all directions at once. It was like a mad version of Italian Mario Karts, seeing who would swerve first, horns honking, brakes squealing and arms waving. Vehicles stopped abruptly without warning to enable conversations across cars. Yet others found perfect parking opportunities by simply stopping wherever they happened to be: centre of an intersection, on top of a roundabout, parking in its most liberal, ad hoc form. It was bonkers, but brilliant at the same time.

A honk behind us caused us to jump and startled us out of our traffic paralysis. We just needed to dive right into the thick of it and hope for the best. If I was religious or had rosary beads, then would have been the time to clutch them tightly in my hands. Geoffrey leant in closer, gripping the steering wheel in a deathly grip, knuckles prominent as we lurched out into the chaos.

'Shit,' I said.

Seeing Vespas flying towards us, Geoffrey slammed one hand on the horn and held it there.

'Why's Dad tooting?' asked Don from the back seat.

'Because he's an Italian driver now,' commented Jan, watching with interest.

Geoffrey's hand came off the horn just long enough to project a middle finger out of the window at an Audi driver before returning to the horn.

'Why did Dad put his finger out of the window?' asked Don, inquisitive as ever.

'It's an Italian greeting,' I heard Jan reply.

I decided help was needed. Quickly winding my window down, I copied the Italians, gesticulating wildly like a crazed lollipop lady managing traffic at the crosswalk.

'What's Mum doing?' asked Don.

'So embarrassing, whatever it is,' said Jan slithering down in her seat.

Holding my hand out to stop traffic and extending my arm in the direction we were going, we proceeded slowly. I alternately glared at black Audis, flapped my arm about and shouted, *'Grazie, grazie,'* until we were safely across. And that was our introduction to driving in Campania. Whenever we forgot the 'Campania way' and accidentally stopped at a red light, tooting horns behind us would snap us back to our new reality. Traffic lights were purely for decoration—pretty colours, but otherwise to be discounted.

Villa Orlandino, when we got there, was a delight: a simple, two-bedroom house on the side of a terraced slope that was gated off from the road above so it was Don-proof. A rooftop terrace had the most spectacular views out to the Tyrrhenian Sea and the tip of the Sorrentine Peninsula. Tiled steps led down to a lower terrace past planter boxes filled with fragrant tomatoes and herbs. From the bottom of the steps, you accessed the cool interior of the villa which was shaded by a row of olive trees, dripping ripe black olives onto the terracotta terrace.

The following morning we headed into the small town of Sant'Agata in search of a homemade pasta shop recommended by the villa owner. Here we were welcomed and looked after by mama. She spoke loudly in rapid Italian, waving her generously proportioned arms around. Mama Agata, as we named her, decided what we would have for dinner. Her strong, tanned arms dished some fresh tomato sauce out of her big cauldron into a container for us to accompany her fresh ravioli. Mama Agata gave us strict instructions on how to cook the ravioli and told us to come back during the week to see her. We did, frequently, possibly every day, but who's counting? Mama's homemade pasta dishes were mouthwateringly delectable. We just showed up and she dished up whatever she decided we were having; there was no arguing with mama, and we loved it.

With dinner sorted we headed to Sorrento for cappuccino and tiramisu before wandering the delightful, narrow cobbled lanes filled with products of the region. The yellow of Sorrento lemons featured heavily in colour, taste and design from candy to soaps, limoncello, fabrics and bright ceramics. There were also a few beggars hustling for cash. We were at first full of sympathy until we saw a supposedly one-legged man hop up to stretch his now two legs. His second leg conveniently folded underneath his coat must have been giving him cramp, poor love. Don stared at him, looking thoughtful. I sensed an embarrassingly frank question coming on. We needed to move off quickly.

Back in the main bustling centre of Sorrento, we came across a double-decker, open-top tourist bus so climbed aboard for an impromptu tour around the Sorrentine Peninsula. From our vantage point at the back of the open-top deck, we could marvel at the scenery and enjoy the fresh breeze. We soon left Sorrento behind and headed out into the terraced headland high above the ocean. As we drove around the narrow, twisty turns of the coast road, suddenly low-hanging vines and branches spilling over rock walls hurtled towards us at high speed. The Brits sitting at the front of the open deck were first in the firing line of the wayward crops. How did we know they were Brits?

'Cor blimey, thut was close, duck yer 'eads up back, luvs,' they called out, chuckling loudly.

We quickly took cover as assorted branches whipped over our heads—olives, grapes and lemons. Clambering back into our seats, those that hadn't been fast enough were left plucking leaves, sticks or olives out of their hair as we all roared with laughter.

'Flippin' 'eck. Duck.' The Brits shouted another warning. We quickly ducked before being slapped in the face by a bundle of leaves, much like a Russian sauna treatment. When we bobbed up again, I couldn't help noticing a perfect, ripe, black, plump olive sitting atop the head of the passenger in front of me.

'Excuse me, sir. There's an olive on your head,' I mumbled to myself, giggling, just because the opportunity to say something like that doesn't come along every day. With that, the olive rolled off the man's head as we lurched around a corner. The mad game of duck and harvest took place while rolling around death-defying cliffs jutting out over a steep drop, horn blaring. We were too busy concentrating on not getting garrotted to worry about the road. There were now enough ripe olives rolling around the top deck to press into a bottle of oil. Needless to say, a good time was had by all. Not a thing was seen of the scenery but we were all now well versed on the local autumn crops of the Sorrentine Peninsula.

On the day we set off to explore Pompeii, we were delayed after stopping in Sant'Agata to call into the bank. We were bamboozled by the Italian propensity to huddle, unsure where to stand or if we were in some sort of invisible queue. We quickly realised that getting served would take time, and that time didn't really matter. What was important was the opportunity to engage in lively conversation at a satisfyingly loud volume with the requisite waving about of hands.

Upon leaving the bank, mama from the pasta shop spied us and rushed out to pat Don's bonny blonde head. '*Buongiorno, buongiorno, ahhh, the bambino,*' she said, patting Don's reluctant head again. Mama informed us that we must now go to the greengrocer's because we needed a zucchini to go with the ragout sauce she was making for our dinner. She went back into her shop to dish out the sauce.

We ducked in to get the zucchini, only to find that zucchini purchasing too involved a lengthy discussion. The greengrocer needed to know exactly how we were going to cook the vegetable to ensure that we weren't going to stuff it up. Finally we dropped the precious pasta, ragout sauce and zucchini safely back home to Villa Orlandino before we set off once more for Pompeii.

As we walked the rough cobbled streets of Pompeii, it was easy to imagine it bustling with Romans and life before the tragic day in AD 79 when Mount Vesuvius erupted, covering the city in ash and preserving it for eternity. Filled with awe, we stepped inside Roman villas inhabited nearly 2,000 years ago. Inside were remnants of lives lived and suddenly ended: tiles and frescos, bathhouses, implements and relics, oil jars and fountains. The ruins of Pompeii included amphitheatres, forums, bakeries, bars and brothels. Given Don's propensity to ask questions, and Jan's willingness to provide him with inappropriate answers, we steered clear of the decorative brothels. These are said to provide a menu of what was on offer in the form of erotic wall paintings—something best avoided when travelling with an inquisitive six-year-old.

We were moved when we viewed the preserved body casts and saw the expressions of horror and pain etched on the faces. It seemed surreal that we could see the result so clearly of an event that took place centuries ago. Calcified layers of ash preserved the form of these victims in the same stance as the moment they were overcome by the pyroclastic flow. We looked at them in hushed silence.

Jan and Don were awestruck by the experience of seeing Pompeii, soaking up all the information. At the souvenir stalls afterwards, they chose some books about Pompeii and a set of different types of lava in a little wooden box. Here Don was fussed over some more by the street vendors. Over a late lunch just outside the gates, we were waited on by a flotilla of gorgeously groomed Italian men who only had eyes for Don. Children, especially boys, are much cherished by Italians. Don was getting a little irritated with all the attention and constantly having his hair ruffled. He just wanted to examine his volcano souvenirs and look at his books in peace without having strangers patting him.

'Why do they keep rubbing Don's head?' asked Jan with a look of distaste. 'It's creepy.'

'They're not paedophiles,' I whispered.

'What's a pedal-pile?' asked Don with interest. Talk about bionic ears!

'No, you don't,' I said, glaring at Jan before she chimed in with a response. Thankfully the waiters arrived with our food and Don was distracted with his Margherita pizza.

SPIES AND STINGERS

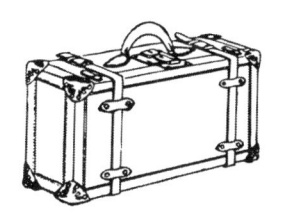

I finally fulfilled a dream to see the Amalfi Coast, with its picture-perfect, pastel villages cascading down to sparkling waters. Terraces were laden with bougainvillea, vivid geraniums, hibiscus and roses. Colourful majolica-tiled church domes adorned each village, picking out the colours of the landscape. Around us echoed the sound of bells ringing, happy laughter, scooters tooting and waves rasping along the pebbles. Shops with pretty, seaside-themed gifts, floaty blue and white fabrics, vibrant ceramics and tiles lined the village streets. Fishing boats bobbed and seafood smells wafted in the air, mingling with the scent of lemons and gelato.

We paddled in Positano, met a Mafia spy then ate lunch with a rat. Let me explain.

After wandering, shopping, photographing and paddling, we sought refuge from the heat in one of Positano's beachside cafés. We were ready for a cappuccino and a refreshing gelato. As we sat there minding our own business, a man looking to be in his 50s, grey-haired and oddly dressed in a dark suit, approached our table and in a posh British accent said, 'Excuse me, do you mind if I join you? I was listening to your conversation. Are you from New Zealand?'

'Yes, we are,' I replied.

'Where do you live there?' he asked.

'Wellington.' OK, I admit it. I would never make a secret agent. I just leak information at the drop of a hat, like a sieve, no torture implements required.

'Oh well, what a coincidence,' he said, sitting himself down. 'I've spent time in New Zealand and have Wellington friends who are quite high up in the government. They're coming to join me next week.'

We introduced ourselves by name though I noticed he didn't offer his but shook all our hands. *He must be blimmin' hot in that ridiculous suit.* Mystery man proceeded to tell us that he was there with his wife, living in Naples on a five-year contract and that he was two years into the job. He stared slowly out towards the sea, lowering his dark sunglasses for effect. I noticed Jan rolling her eyes.

'See those Italian Navy ships?' he asked.

'Yes,' said Geoffrey, following his gaze.

'They're patrolling up and down the coast,' he said.

Well obviously, I thought and noticed Jan roll her eyes again and look at her watch. Don studiously licked his gelato, savouring the flavour, and completely ignored this new and quite frankly odd intruder at our table.

Before waiting for a response, the man continued telling us in a conspiratorial tone all about what the Mafia were up to in the area—people smuggling, drug smuggling, gun smuggling—you name it, he spilt the beans on it in long and laborious detail. Then he made a show of looking all around him before finishing in a low voice, 'So I'm here to keep an eye on them.'

Don took a deep and noisy slurp through his straw, sucking up the last of his milkshake. Shhhuulllppp.

Well, you're a bit of a blabbermouth for a spy. And what self-respecting spy is going to walk around in a dark suit and mirrored glasses? Amateur! It was all very intriguing but we had a coast to explore and excused ourselves.

On the way out, Jan hissed at me, 'I bet you made eye contact with that nutter, Mum. I've told you. Stop looking at people. Look at the ground. You keep attracting weirdos.'

Who? Me?

After we'd explored Amalfi, which was less crowded than Positano, Don splashed around at the water's edge, examining rocks for signs of pumice and lava and building volcanos. I watched him and rested my tired feet while Geoffrey dutifully accompanied Jan around the shops. We ate a late lunch in an open-sided café set on a platform out over the crystal-clear water. Colourful fishing boats gently swayed in the current beside us and the slight sea breeze helped to cool us off. Just after the waiter took our order, Don announced matter-of-factly, 'There's a rat.'

'Where?' we all screamed in unison. Geoffrey, Jan and I automatically lifted our legs off the ground, fearfully scanning the floor. Alarming thoughts of dining in a café rife with rodents running around flashed into my head.

'There,' said Don, pointing below us to the water. Our eyes followed the direction he was pointing and, sure enough, there was ratty. Big, fat, bloated, decidedly dead ratty was bobbing around idly at the water's edge. He rolled in and out with each wave. We watched, mesmerised, and wondered if we should leave. Too late. Our lunch arrived and was delicious. Don stuck to a classic Margherita pizza, while the three of us enjoyed seafood ravioli in a delicate creamy sauce. Ratty continued with his dead-rat surfing routine just below us while we ate. This caused a fair few fits of hushed giggling and rodent jokes over lunch.

Before long it was time to drag ourselves, our tired feet and sunburnt faces homewards towards Villa Orlandino. As we drove along the treacherous Amalfi Coast road, the setting sun turned the Tyrrhenian Sea into waves of glittering gold. The road was little more than a narrow ledge cut out of the cliffside, snaking high above the ocean in a continuous series of tight and blind corners. It's feared by many and known to be a challenging drive.

'This is awesome,' blurted Geoffrey in his excitement. 'It's like a whole series of racetrack chicanes all rolled into one.' He was having a thoroughly good time reliving the motorbike racing days of his youth.

'You're actually not that good a driver, Dad,' stated Jan. 'You rode your motorbike into the harbour.' We all spluttered out loud, even Geoffrey, as we pictured the time he and his bike sailed through the air, landing with an almighty splash in the water.

That night I got a signal on the cell phone from the roof terrace to call my mother in New Zealand.

'Guess what?' I said. 'We met a Mafia spy today.'

'Oh, for goodness' sake. What have I told you about not talking to strangers?' was the response.

The next morning we had a boat trip to Capri so we left our car in a port garage at Sorrento. By the time we returned at the end of the day, we noticed we had a flat tyre. Geoffrey put the spare on but the main tyre needed repairing and the car was due for a service. At 11 a.m. the next morning, Geoffrey went into Sant'Agata. The car rental company had arranged to send someone from a garage in Sorrento to meet him in the car park.

Back at Villa Orlandino, Don was roaming the garden watching the friendly geckos, picking tomatoes for me and being a volcano. Jan caught up on some school work after a busy week. Pompeii covered history, classics and geography all rolled into one, while learning Italian words was an ongoing lesson for all of us. I prepared a lunch of Don's freshly picked tomatoes and basil from the garden on toast, sprinkled with olive oil. If mama asked, it was bruschetta.

Meanwhile up the road in the village, the garage man had arrived. He didn't speak a word of English and Geoffrey's Italian only stretched to ordering a pizza. The mechanic pulled out a phone and rang his boss at the garage who seemingly dashed next door to the bus depot ticket booth. Bustling aside the queue of customers, he thrust the phone at the poor man while rapidly explaining what he needed to say to the idiot on the other end of the phone. The message was conveyed. The tyre wasn't repairable; they would order a spare. Geoffrey was to drive down to Sorrento the next morning and leave the car with them for a couple of hours. They would fit the new tyre and do the service.

Geoffrey returned home and after lunch we drove down to Marina del Cantone, the beach below us, tucked in beneath the cliffs at the bottom of a sharp, zigzagging road. The pebbly beach was dotted with bright-orange sun umbrellas looking like neat rows of nasturtiums positioned next to the water. The fishing village of Nerano encircled the small bay with a row of bars and simple cafés offering traditional seafood.

We paid a few euros to use the sunbeds beside the glass-like water. Nothing stirred; beads of perspiration formed on our bodies; the sea was becalmed. Geoffrey headed into the water to cool off. I dozed in the heat, listening to the water sucking gently over the pebbles.

Suddenly I heard a shout from the water and sat up. *Shit, is it a shark?* I was guilty of not scanning for fins. *Has Geoffrey been taken?* I couldn't see any spreading pool of red blood in the sea but there he was, thrashing about in the water, screaming. The kids sat up and stared at their father who was slowly making his way towards the shore in between bouts of grabbing at his body and yelling obscenities.

'What's wrong with Dad?' asked Jan.

'No idea, but he's definitely still got two arms and at least one leg attached.'

'He's so embarrassing; everyone's staring at him. He's making a right spectacle of himself.'

With that, Geoffrey clambered out of the surf at our feet and climbed the shingle bank. Three sets of eyes stared at him with interest. He continued to slap at his chest and arms, writhing around. 'Arrrggghhh, bloody jellyfish. I've been stung,' he groaned in agony.

He wasn't exaggerating. Giant, impressive red welts laced his torso and arms.

'There were tons of the blighters,' he grumbled.

The kids admired his battle scars, deeply impressed.

'Dad, you're as red as lava,' said a wide-eyed Don, cleverly comparing his father to a volcano.

The beach was cancelled and the rest of the afternoon was spent plucking gelatinous tentacles from Geoffrey's burning skin.

That evening at Villa Orlandino, we dined on mama's home cooking before heading up to the rooftop terrace together to watch the sunset. Once the sun had dipped below the horizon in a spectacular blaze of glory, bats appeared, swooping and diving and catching pesky mosquitoes; an owl hooted nearby in the olive trees; a few neighbourhood dogs were barking. Geoffrey scratched at his inflamed skin.

The following morning Geoffrey drove down to the garage and the mechanic promptly dragged him next door to the bus depot. Tourists were once again shunted aside as Geoffrey was delivered to the ticket booth and the poor man who had found himself unexpectedly involved in our business. The mechanic let off a volley of rapid-fire Italian which the ticket seller conveyed in English. The mechanic was most apologetic. The spare tyre hadn't arrived but would hopefully be there in the afternoon. He would do the service now but Geoffrey would need to return at the end of the day for them to fit the tyre.

Later Jan went for a ride with her dad to get the new tyre fitted while I cleaned the villa ready for changeover day departure the next morning. Don was pinned down to stay inside with me until he had written up his journal and finished his school work. With that done, he was released to continue his volcano games on the rooftop deck, the neighbour conveniently providing him with a smoky prop for his antics by burning autumn grapevine trimmings. Don's volcanic eruption noises intermittently punctuated the air, making me laugh.

Finally Geoffrey and Jan returned and we all sat down for our last Amalfi Coast dinner in Villa Orlandino. None of us wanted to leave; we would miss mama's home cooking.

The jellyfish stings hadn't finished with Geoffrey though. When we returned home a week later, they were still swollen and inflamed. The Amalfi Coast stingers cost Geoffrey not one but two visits to a doctor after becoming infected. This had been a holiday with a true sting in its tail.

2012

FRANCE AND ITALY

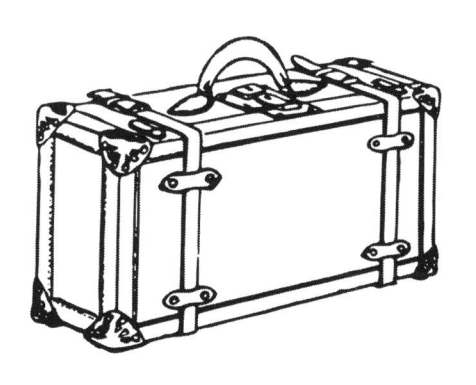

CATHAR CASTLE SPECTRE

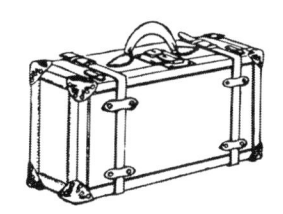

Our 2006 trip had only served to whet our appetite for more travel and given us a bad case of itchy feet. Over the next few years, I studied and qualified as an early childhood teacher while working and saving every penny. Finally, with the blessing of supportive employers and the school principal, our family was ready to travel again. This time we knew not to try and cover such vast distances, instead trying to stay in each location for a week, giving us time to explore each place properly.

And so it was that in 2012, we found ourselves spending a week in a medieval stone house just below the Church of Saint-Saturnin in the village of Vernet-les-Bains amid the foothills of the Pyrenees. This was the first week of our European adventure which would take us across Southern France and Italy. Don was now twelve and Jan had just turned nineteen.

When I looked at websites of things to do in the Languedoc, magnificent-looking Cathar castles popped up repeatedly. My curiosity was piqued. All I knew was that in the 12th century, a new religion called Catharism flourished in the area. Labelled as heretics, the Cathars were pursued in a violent crusade ordered by the Catholic church. Cathars and their followers took refuge in castles and fortified towns in the foothills of the Pyrenees. Many of these spectacular, romantic and poignant medieval castles are now open to visitors. Not having castles in New Zealand, or buildings much older than 100 years, exploring Cathar castles went to the top of our wish list.

Our first and much-anticipated Cathar castle was Château de Puilaurens, located just outside of its namesake village of Puilaurens in Southwest France. We followed a narrow road from the village that took us to the car park entrance for climbing up to the castle on foot. A rocky and dusty track led us uphill along a pine-forest slope, obscuring the castle from our sight. The wooden walking poles that we'd bought a couple of days earlier in Villefranche-sur-Mer came in handy as we traversed up and over large rocks and stone steps worn smooth by centuries of wear. It appeared that we were the only visitors there; we hadn't seen anyone around and there were no other cars in the car park. This just made it all the more special. Fancy having an entire castle to ourselves to explore.

The castle loomed above us as we emerged from the forest, jutting from a rocky outcrop. A silhouette of towers and rampart crenellations appeared at 697 metres high. The castle's defensive walls appeared to grow out of the very rock it was built upon, rising sentinel above us. Menacing arrow slits, where once arrows would have rained down upon us as we advanced, dotted the stone walls. Then the steep climb began, up a narrow and once heavily defended stone staircase zigzagging tightly, hugging the side of the cliff.

The kids surged on ahead, disappearing from sight. I looked upwards, checking progress, and could see their heads bobbing along far above. A pair of peregrine falcons swooped over the castle. Breathing heavily and leaning on the stick for support, I pressed on up each gigantic stone tread, stopping periodically to catch my breath. *This castle had better be worth the effort.* Geoffrey waited patiently and eventually we could see the arched entry allowing access to within the castle walls. That was if we made it past the defensive barbican (a fortified gateway) containing remnants of the murder hole, a gap in the ceiling of the gateway through which the defenders could fire, throw or pour harmful substances or objects such as rocks, arrows, scalding water or boiling oil down onto attackers.

Jan and Don were leaning over the edge above, calling to us to hurry up. Geoffrey and I reached the top and stepped through the barbican protecting the entrance, finding ourselves in an enclosed grassed courtyard with a few straggly trees. Towering stone walls bordered it, flanked by two smaller round keeps at the far end. Having entered along the western wall, the main castle structure and the largest of the round towers were to our left. A series of wooden ramps and stone stairs led to the internal areas of the castle and up to the parapets.

Geoffrey, Jan and Don eagerly set off up the stairs towards the towers and parapets to explore. I went to follow them but something made me stop. I don't know why as I normally love to wander inside castles, especially after all the effort of getting up there. I told them to carry on. I would wait for them in the grassed courtyard. They weren't really listening, having bounded off, eager to investigate the interior.

Inside they followed a maze of narrow corridors, glancing through arrow slits, taking in the sheer drop beneath as if they'd been plunged back into the Middle Ages. They stepped carefully onto the crumbling ramparts where I could see them from below, facing out towards the valley, admiring the panorama. *Why didn't I just join them? This is silly*, I thought, wavering.

Before I could change my mind, the sun disappeared and the temperature suddenly dropped. Looking up I noticed dark, ominous-looking storm clouds gathering. I shivered; the atmosphere was changing somehow. It felt different. Moving away from the entrance where the murder hole was located, I heard a blood-curdling scream. The hairs stood up on the back of my neck. An image flashed through my mind as if from nowhere: the fleeting and horrifying image of a woman leaping from the castle, wearing a long dress.

I quickly glanced in the direction my family had gone, relieved to see three heads still standing up on the parapet, admiring the view and taking photos. To my surprise, they didn't appear startled or concerned about the blood-curdling scream. They hadn't turned or looked around and yet I knew what I'd just heard. I glanced back through the archway. There was no one coming up the track below and no one else within the castle walls. I was confused. Was it my imagination? Maybe the falcons calling?

Hastily moving away from the stone walls, I walked into the centre of the courtyard, sitting down on the grass to steady my shaky legs. A strong feeling of anxiety and sadness washed over me and I just wanted to get out of there. I didn't know anything about Château de Puilaurens or its history but after what had just happened, I was intrigued.

The kids arrived back and I asked them if they'd heard a woman's scream. They responded with blank stares. Confused, I checked if they'd seen anyone else around, but no, they hadn't. Bored with their mother's stupid questions, they zoomed off to continue their tour of the castle. After catching up with Geoffrey, they headed around the courtyard's perimeter towards the smaller towers while searching for any hidden passageways.

A little while later, our visit was thankfully cut short as dark clouds closed in fast. A light mist began to drape the castle walls and the air grew chilly. The wind picked up. A storm was coming. I didn't want to be caught out there; we needed to leave.

As we made our way back down the track, we heard a crack of thunder and rain began to fall, making the stones precariously slippery in the wet. We were thankful for the steadying support of our walking sticks. I strode on as fast as I dared, trying to put as much distance as possible between myself and Château de Puilaurens. I didn't look back. By the time we reached the car, my mood had lifted and I breathed in deeply. We stopped at the little ticket booth at the car park to buy a brochure about the castle. I needed to know more about this place.

Back in our village house that afternoon, I sprawled out on the rickety bed, reading the brochure. Outside the bedroom, grapes hung in fat bunches, supported by a trellis, their sweet scent and purple stickiness attracting strange, hovering bumblebees that looked like miniature hummingbirds. Don was on the terrace, staring at them closely.

Turning my attention back to the brochure, I learnt that of all of the many Cathar castles, Puilaurens is the only one that appears to experience regular, documented ghostly phenomena. It started life peacefully enough in the 10th century, occupied by an order of monks before the King of Aragon acquired it in 1162. Château de Puilaurens later went through a more turbulent period, involved in territorial battles between France and Spain due to its ideal defensive location, sitting atop a high rocky outcrop with vast views from its battlements. By far its most violent period was during the time of the Cathars who rejected the material world and many of the trappings of the dominant Roman Catholic faith, refusing to contribute financially to the Catholic purse. Unsurprisingly, this didn't go down well with the Pope at the time. He retaliated, declaring Cathars to be heretics, sending a holy army to wipe them out. It resulted in the slaughter of 600,000 men, women and children during this war.

Château de Puilaurens had its fair share of gruesome tragedy and bloodshed. During one attempted massacre, many Cathars, including women and children, fled a nearby town to seek refuge within the walls of the castle. Here they were reportedly trapped and brutally murdered by soldiers following orders from Catholic leaders. Not surprisingly there have been numerous accounts over the years of strange feelings and ghostly occurrences. But the most reported is the story of a mysterious lady in white, purported to be Blanche of Bourbon, who is said to float around the castle and along the battlements.

One of the towers bears her name and is called the White Lady Tower, the one next to where we entered the castle walls. Princess Blanche stayed in Puilaurens in 1353 on her way to Spain and was to be married to the King of Castile, known as Peter the Cruel. Doesn't he sound a catch? She was only fourteen. Her new husband rejected this arranged marriage, abandoned her three days after their wedding and had her locked up in the castle of Arévalo in Spain. Poor Blanche died eight years later, still a prisoner, on the orders of her husband.

Blanche supposedly haunts the grounds of Puilaurens as a white, misty apparition. This seems an unlikely assumption to me; she wasn't murdered there and had only been a temporary visitor. It would seem far more plausible for sightings of a ghostly figure of a woman to be one of the trapped and terrified Cathars who either jumped from the castle walls to escape the soldiers or was pushed. I guess the story of Princess Blanche makes for better reading.

Learning of this tragic history made what I'd experienced seem all the more real. Why did my family not hear the scream too? Geoffrey came in to grab his book off the bedside cabinet.

'I think it was a Cathar ghost I heard scream,' I announced.

'Oh, for God's sake,' muttered Geoffrey, hastily retreating.

Is it possible that I have a talent for attracting trouble and weirdness, not just living but dead? I pondered. I was disappointed that I'd slogged all the way up that steep track and then not managed to explore inside the castle.

'Mum, come and look. I think it really is a hummingbird,' called Don from the terrace.

Over the following week, we visited several other magnificent Cathar castles which I did get to explore without experiencing anything remotely unusual. But I've never forgotten Puilaurens. It's amazing to think that the castle's stone walls and towers have stood through centuries of tragic history. If only they could speak, but preferably not to Denise.

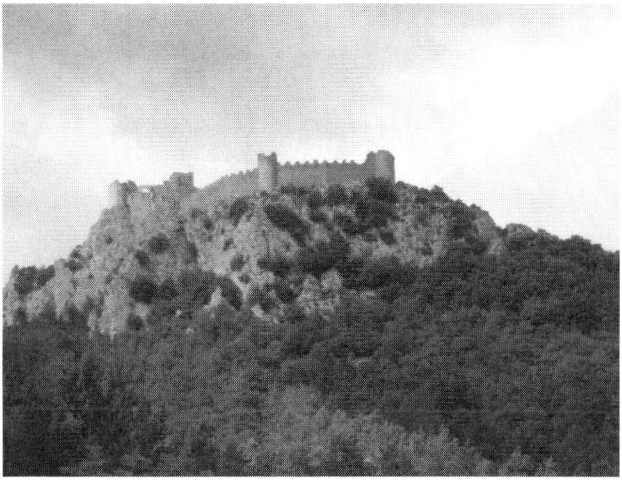

WE'VE BEEN WATCHING YOU

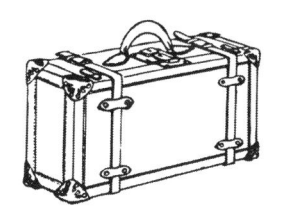

As we left the Cathar castles behind, we endured bloody battles of our own in Durban-Corbières. Our holiday rental seemed determined to leave us scarred by multiple accidents inside its walls. Within hours of arrival, Geoffrey's glasses had been forcibly mashed into his face; a plug was impaled upon his foot; a wooden coat rack fell on Jan's head; Don jammed his finger in a door and I bruised my leg on the bed. So we were relieved to move on to Provence to recover and prepare for re-entry into the Italian way of life. Before we knew it, changeover day was upon us with a drive of over eight hours from Provence to Tuscany. The destination was a quaint hilltop village called Panzano, roughly halfway between Florence and Siena.

When we reached it at the end of the day, we viewed Panzano's central piazza a grand total of eight times. The village residents were gathered there, enjoying the daily *passeggiata*, an age-old evening ritual conducted all over Italy, a gentle and slow stroll through the main streets of town, usually culminating at the piazza. While villagers sat, chatted, strolled and enjoyed a crisp glass of vino, the Hayhursts drove through the middle of them, again and again, and again. Yes, of course we were lost. The trusty satnav was insisting that our destination was right here, but where, exactly, was here?

Heads turned, eyes strained, following us questioningly. Three roads led into the piazza. To keep the residents on their toes, our car appeared from a different direction each time, trying multiple direction combinations but ultimately taking us precisely nowhere. On our fourth bypass, the kids ducked down on the back seat, mortified with embarrassment at the laughing, pointing, staring and chuckling villagers. To mix things up a little, we next came through the one-way entrance into the piazza the wrong way but Geoffrey was beyond caring and beyond reason by this point.

Within the car a domestic was in full swing. Geoffrey was cursing; I was to blame and the kids had had enough. We entered Panzano, drove right past our rental without realising it and left Panzano. We circled Panzano. We came at Panzano from all angles, each time driving right past our rental. By the time we located it, a family was standing at their window in the flat above our apartment. I think they'd received a phone call from the village square. As we finally pulled in, I'm sure everyone in the piazza broke into applause, clinking their glasses in celebration. The neighbours upstairs stepped out onto their balcony and stood staring directly at us, not looking away, just staring.

'They're creepy,' whispered Jan.

'Like zombies,' commented Don.

Thankfully the owner arrived and introduced himself—what a welcoming and generous man. He gave us a homemade blueberry and walnut tart and a bottle of red wine he'd made then left us to settle in. The downstairs apartment was spacious and homely: tiled floors, high ceilings and shuttered windows. The street entrance faced the village but from the bedrooms the views stretched out over the rolling Tuscan countryside below. Geoffrey and the kids went to explore the house and garden while I sorted the groceries before preparing a quick dinner of pizza, salad and that morning's baguette bought in Provence. I'm sure you can guess what was for dessert. Oh, and if anyone thinks I sound like a '50s housewife, Geoffrey does all the driving and I'm sure you've gathered by now that driving us lot around foreign countries all day, aided by lunatic satnavs, is a stressful task. My end of the bargain is to do the cooking and I'm more than happy with that.

That night when everyone was tucked up in bed, exhausted after the long day, I noticed huge flashes of blinding light through the shutters. Getting up to investigate, I peered out across the rolling Chianti countryside below. Flashes of lightning streaking across the night sky were lighting up the horizon. Deafening thunder reverberated around our wee hilltop village. Rain lashed at the windows. The commotion woke Geoffrey. There was scant chance of us sleeping amid this racket. The kids, however, snoozed on.

The next morning Jan and Don, refreshed from a sound night's sleep, were up and about before us. A strong hit of Italian-style espresso sorted us out to wander the short distance into the village piazza, which we were now very familiar with. As it was market day, the square was alive with busy activity, all set around the central fountain and a large, shady tree. We found the corner store, where the grocer seemed to know who we were when he greeted us with a comment of, 'Good to see you again.' *That seems odd. He must have mistaken us for someone else*, we thought. After purchasing a few groceries and a local Chianti wine, we wandered the market stalls, observing with interest.

Before us was a humming, vibrant scene. Italians greeted each other exuberantly, chatting, gesticulating and calling out. Cars stopped in random places for the drivers to strike up conversations; horns tooted. Fashion-conscious Italians strutted, displaying deep tans and good grooming. The smell of leather, rotisserie chicken and expensive perfume filled the air. Young men stood in groups watching the young ladies, cigarette smoke rising. Nonnas and poppas sat grouped on seats, all headscarves and sensible cardigans. Stallholders hollered as housewives competed to be heard. We sat by the fountain under the shade of the old tree, eating gelatos, taking it all in and smiling. Life was good; this was la dolce vita.

Gelatos finished, we wandered across the road to visit Dario Cecchini's famous butchery. Dario is a Tuscan legend from a family of eight generations of butchers. A visit to his butchery is a must when in the area to see this larger-than-life, colourful character. Before even stepping through the door, we were met by 100 decibels of AC/DC blaring out. Inside Dario's, glasses of luscious plonk were proffered. Trays of mouthwatering Tuscan snacks circulated for tasting alongside the wine we were sipping. With tastebuds occupied, we feasted our eyes on the colourful works of art adorning every wall, featuring Dario's beloved Tuscany. AC/DC continued to pummel away in the background.

At the centre of it all was Dario himself, holding court like a conductor, working the room, controlling all the components of this sensory orchestra while slicing wondrous slabs of juicy Chianina steak. Deciding on black-pepper beef stew, we stepped forward to the counter. Brightly dressed, ruddy complexion and booming voice, head nodding in time to AC/DC, the legend himself served us and chuckled.

'I see you found where you were going then,' he shouted over the top of the music, eyes twinkling.

We looked at him blankly.

'The Frogs from the silver Peugeot,' he called out.

'We're not Frogs; we're Kiwis,' I said indignantly.

'Aaaah, zee car has zee French plates, you see, *oui oui*,' he pointed out, roaring with laughter at his own joke.

We giggled with embarrassment that he'd obviously witnessed our woeful entry into Panzano. We wandered home, clutching our precious goods. As we reached our apartment, the upstairs neighbours' curtain twitched and they all stepped out onto the balcony. Mum, dad and adult son stood there, staring at us directly, not smiling, not waving, not greeting, just blank stares.

'Shit, they're creepy,' said Geoffrey.

'Zombies,' iterated Don.

'Better make sure the doors are locked tonight,' I commented before calling out a cheerful *'buongiorno'* and waving. There was no response.

Geoffrey and Jan retired for a siesta while Don went out to explore in the garden and I, well, I did a load of washing and prepared a salad to go with our black-pepper beef stew. After dinner we went for a stroll into the village. Jan had noticed a leather shop just along from our villa and it was now open. Inside, a smiling young woman who introduced herself as Simona greeted us warmly and enquired if we were enjoying our stay in Panzano. I asked her how she knew we were staying there.

'I recognise you,' she answered, grinning.

We looked confused so she explained.

'You have the silver Peugeot with the French licence plate,' she said matter-of-factly. She laughed. 'Most of the village knows who you are. We all saw you driving through our piazza the night you arrived. You drove by so many times; it was ever so funny. We thought you were a family of French idiots.'

'Family of idiots indeed,' I muttered indignantly on the way home.

As we approached our villa, we heard the familiar sound of the upstairs door sliding open.

'Oh no, here come The Munsters again,' said Jan.

And sure enough, they all filed out and stood at the railing, staring.

'They're so weird,' said Don.

'Oh, this is ridiculous,' I whispered. 'Geoffrey, do something.'

'Like what?' he muttered. We shrugged and marched inside, making sure we locked the door behind us.

Another beautiful, blue-sky Tuscan day greeted us next morning as we set off for Siena. As we reversed out of the drive in the car, The Munsters all came out to stare again.

'We could line up and stare back,' suggested Geoffrey.

'That would soon be all around the village and they already think we're a bunch of idiots.' I laughed. But in all honesty, the family of loons upstairs was starting to freak me out. What invisible force kept attracting weirdos? Could it really be me?

After parking, we approached the historic centre of Siena, walking up a steep, medieval lane before stepping into the famous Piazza del Campo. We stopped and stared. I could see why it's considered one of the most beautiful medieval squares in all of Italy. The entire scallop shell-shaped piazza was ringed with magnificent buildings in complementary shades of terracotta and fringed with a sea of red awnings adorning outdoor cafés.

At its centre, terracotta-brick paving radiated out from the Palazzo Pubblico building, forming the scallop-shell shape. The enormous, arched marble façade of Siena's communal palace, with the impressive Torre del Mangia bell tower rising from one end, dominated the space opposite us. Behind Piazza del Campo was a glimpse of Siena's famous 13th-century black and white Gothic-style cathedral, the largest in all of Italy.

We decided to visit the cathedral first while it wasn't too busy. As we left the piazza, the enormous scale of this striped marble cathedral in the shape of a Latin cross became apparent. Just approaching it was breathtaking. At the ticket counter, we were told the inlaid marble mosaic floors are only uncovered for one month a year; this was the last day to see them.

In the vast interior, the columns continued the black and white marble-striped motif. As we looked up, we saw solidly proportioned busts of past religious men of Siena gazing down upon us. Overcome by the Gothic cathedral's immensity, I took a seat on the nearest pew, absorbing the sheer scale of the interior and layer upon layer of complex colour and design.

My gaze was drawn upwards towards the vaulted roof, decorated in blue with golden stars. Below me the deeply intricate mosaic floor represented colourful scenes from the Old Testament. Approaching the Carrara marble pulpit, I noticed the light catching the circular, stained-glass window depicting the Last Supper. The church's interior was overflowing with treasures by famous Italian artists and sculptors.

Flickering candles added to the magical atmosphere as we slowly moved through the interior in silence.

After this extraordinary experience, we strolled back to the Piazza del Campo where we sat contentedly, eating pizza and people-watching at an outdoor café underneath a bright-red awning. A crisp Chianti wine complemented this most magnificent setting.

After lunch Geoffrey and Don set off to climb the 14th-century medieval Torre del Mangia. Around 400 narrow, steep steps covered in pigeon droppings led them up a claustrophobic climb of 90 metres to the ancient bell tower. Once at the top, after getting their breath back, they were rewarded with a pigeon's eye view out over the magnificent Piazza del Campo, Siena and beyond to the Tuscan countryside.

Jan and I explored the treasures held within the immense 13th-century Palazzo Pubblico. We wandered, spellbound. Every bit of the high, vaulted ceilings were works of art covered in gilded and colourful frescos. The walls, dripping in tapestries or artworks of an unimaginable scale, depicted battle scenes between Siena and Florence. Exquisite marble statues, silky smooth to the touch, appeared tangibly real—utter beauty everywhere we looked. Meeting up with the boys again, we sat in the piazza, cooling off on a typically warm Tuscan afternoon with refreshing ice-cold drinks. What an unforgettable day it had been.

THE GYPSY CURSE BEGINS

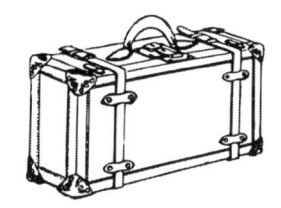

*A*t the end of another sultry, golden autumn day, I sat sipping a Chianti wine. Jan had her nose buried in some English fashion magazines we'd found that day while Don explored the garden for lizards and Geoffrey snored in the background while I wrote.

That morning we'd explored the nearby town of Greve in Chianti where I'd set up a secret rendezvous on a quiet, unassuming little back street. We parked and approached an unmarked building and pressed a buzzer to be admitted to the clandestine underworld of Gino Ferruzzi.

We were led up a flight of stairs by an elegantly dressed woman who introduced herself as Rosa. She unlocked a door to admit us to the inner sanctum with its delicious smell of leather and money. Welcome to a little-known factory where they handmake top-quality belts, wallets, handbags, jackets and other Italian leather creations for Gucci.

Behind a second locked door, we were allowed in to view, touch and even try on some of the Gucci collection. We were the only people there; it felt exclusive and exciting. Rosa explained that while most of their creations are for Gucci, they put their own Gino Ferruzzi label on a small portion of the leather goods to sell to the public. In the factory beneath our feet, they'd been producing fine leather handcrafts in keeping with ancient Tuscan traditions for over twenty years.

Afterwards in the back seat of the car, the kids excitedly discussed and admired their small leather purchases, thrilled with them. Later that night, in the absence of TV or internet, they called a 'leather meeting' for us to examine what they'd bought. Geoffrey and I rolled our eyes but played along.

After leaving the factory, we drove a short distance to Monteriggioni, a 13th-century walled village. Built upon a natural hillock by the Sienese, its medieval fortifications and watchtowers were used as a front line in their wars against Florence. After parking outside the circular walls, we approached Monteriggioni from below, noticing the impressive stone towers neatly spaced along the ramparts. Silvery-green olive trees cloaked the sloping hill beneath the stone wall. Access to the village was through an impressive, stone-arched gate.

It turned out this day was a beer festival. The main piazza was festooned with colourful beer tents exuding aromas of hops. Geoffrey's eyes lit up at the thought of all that delicious beer. But alas he was quickly dragged away. Our first stop was the tourist office where we gained access to a small museum of medieval armour. Don's eyes glinted. He tried on all manner of cumbersome suits of armour, chain-link vests and hoods, thick enough to stop an arrow from piercing the skin. There were weapons too, so soon Don was thrusting swords and daggers, aiming a crossbow, jabbing a lance and a barbed wooden stick, his eyes taking on a menacing look. All his practice with plastic toy daggers and swords when he was younger had finally come to fruition; we had to drag the bloodthirsty little blighter out of there.

We purchased tickets allowing us to climb the rickety wooden steps to reach the top of the rampart walls which provided views of the surrounding Chianti region, miles of undulating hills liberally dotted with Italian cypress, olives and grapevines. We explored part of the ramparts and towers before being lured back to ground level by tantalising glimpses of little boutiques seen from above.

By the time we'd admired the local Tuscan arts, crafts, wine and food products, we were ready for some lunch. Piazza Roma was bordered by a Romanesque church and Renaissance-style buildings housing restaurants and bars, and the outdoor cafés were joined by an abundance of beer tents overflowing with jovial visitors. It seemed a happy atmosphere. But all was not well with everyone, as we were about to find out.

After we'd sat down at a table in the main square, a waiter served us who can only be described as an Italian version of Basil Fawlty. Customer service just wasn't his vibe on this day. Geoffrey and I ordered the bruschetta to start with and asked for a *'primo piatto'*, or first course, but as our main. We were just not hungry enough for an Italian-sized main course. Don asked for a *'primo piatto'* plus a main course, hungry after all that enthusiastic, murderous activity. Jan's order was a simple sandwich off another menu that the waiter had given us.

Well, the poor waiter, who, to be fair, had had a pretty busy morning thanks to the beer festival, nearly blew a gasket. He had an apoplectic outburst, gibbering at us in loud, rapid Italian, waving his arms about and stabbing violently with his pencil at his notepad before swiping our menus off us and dramatically throwing them with force onto the next table. With that, he flounced off to the kitchen in a flummox, still muttering loudly to himself.

We sat there, mouths open, looking at each other in amazement that our order could have caused such a reaction.

'Well, somebody's a little tetchy today,' said Geoffrey.

Hushed laughter erupted around our table, mingled with snorts. Tears ran down my cheeks.

'What do you think he was saying?' asked Don.

I took a guess. 'You've made a complete mockery of my menu, you clueless foreign twits.'

'Shh, Mum, he's coming back,' said Jan, and we all sat, poker-faced, trying not to look at each other.

BANG! He slammed the food down in front of us with dramatic effect, making us jump in unison. I bit my lip, trying not to laugh. Basil Fawlty of course brought all the courses out at once just to make a point of our stupidity. He made rapid return journeys, each time banging the dishes down with force and offering us murderous looks. Finally our table was groaning under the weight of plates of bruschetta, extra-enormous *primi piatti* of wild-boar tagliatelle, Jan's sandwich and Don's pizza main, which was big enough for six people. Basil looked smugly at the piles of food, clicked his heels together and marched off.

'Oh heck.' I groaned. 'We can't leave any. There's no way I'm giving him the satisfaction. Jan, you'll just have to help us eat it.'

And do you know what? That mercenary little madam did. She saw an opportunity to make some cash and flipping well charged us €10 in exchange for her eating half a pizza. What a cheek. But we would consume every last crumb, even if our bellies exploded. There was a principle at stake. I just couldn't remember precisely what that principle was. But Basil was certainly not going to have the last laugh.

'Now, eat up.' I groaned.

After lunch, bellies bulging and Geoffrey too full even to contemplate a beer, we decided exercise was required to aid digestion. We plodded our way back to the entrance to the ramparts, deciding to climb back up to the top of the battlement walls. It would be fun to complete an entire 570-metre circuit of the walls and all fourteen towers. That was if the rickety platform could hold our combined weight.

But something odd was happening to the residents of Monteriggioni; they were behaving in a most peculiar fashion. Was it the Denise effect? This time the Italian lady taking the tickets to let people access the ramparts was having an outlandish meltdown. She was screaming rudely at some poor American tourists and gesticulating madly. Geoffrey stood awkwardly, waiting for the fighting to stop so that he could show her our tickets. The kids and I took a seat to watch the free entertainment. With our overly stuffed stomachs, we didn't even require popcorn. Full and lethargic in the heat, we languished alongside other spectators. An American lady sitting next to me shuffled closer and said loudly in an impressively broad-sounding drawl, 'Sweet Jaysssus, don't mess with herrr. I think she's a gypseeey. I think she already done put a currrse on us, an' she'll likely put one on y'all too.'

I raised my eyebrows at this information and watched with even more interest. Was the angry lady a gypsy? Why was she so disgruntled?

The Italian (possibly gypsy) lady was still hollering and now refused Geoffrey's nervously proffered ticket. She snatched it, ripped it in shreds and tossed it in the air. Geoffrey wisely retreated, waving an imaginary white flag. The angry lady marched into her little ticket booth and slammed the door with a bang.

'Guess we're not going up the ramparts then,' commented Jan.

'It's probably just as well. With the amount we've eaten, it would be like a re-enactment of Humpty Dumpty sat on a wall,' I said.

'Who're you calling Humpty?' muttered Jan indignantly.

'It's the gypsy currrse,' drawled Don in his bestest American accent.

'Let's go,' said Geoffrey. 'These people are bonkers.'

'Not yet, Dad. I've got ten euros to spend first,' said Jan sweetly.

And so began our family legend of the gypsy curse; it all started in Monteriggioni. From this day forward, whenever facing yet another travel disaster, Don always blamed it on the gypsy curse.

The following day, we set off to visit the hilltop village of Montalcino, where it's a must to explore the popular fortress, built in 1361. After centuries of battles, it's now a monument with a view of the Val d'Orcia. Stepping out onto the battlement walls, I hesitated. It appeared much higher from up there than it did from below, and it was so narrow. My confidence faltered. But without pause, I gritted my teeth and set off towards the middle of the wall, staring straight ahead, gripping the sides and not looking down. When I reached the middle, I turned proudly to pose for a photograph, which was when I realised my horrid family had seen me as nothing more than an obstacle and gone in the opposite direction.

The wall was only one person wide, narrow and, oh shit, I made the mistake of looking down. No, no, no. My poor legs turned to jelly. I slunk down, crouching as low as I could behind the stone edge where I couldn't see the drop on either side of me. I would have dropped to my knees if I didn't have a stuffed knee. So there I crouched, knees bent, palms resting on my thighs, butt out, not so much crouching tiger as crouching big bird squatting on a nest. I looked like I was straining to lay a big fat egg.

'Ha ha, Mum looks like Humpty Dumpty now,' said Jan, pointing and laughing. I guess she was right; I was a rotund blob squatting in the middle of a rock wall. I just hoped this Humpty Dumpty didn't have a great fall. The family had done a full circuit, ending up in front of me, wanting to get past to go back down the tower stairs.

'Get up,' said Geoffrey impatiently. 'What on earth are you doing crouched down like that?'

'I don't like it,' I wailed pathetically.

'Mum, you're so embarrassing. Get off the wall,' said Don matter-of-factly.

'We're hungry,' said Jan. 'Get down and stop causing trouble.'

And so I began the shuffling wobble of shame back along the battlement wall, head down and bum sticking out behind me, towards the tower and my source of escape—the stairs. Ahead of me, an understandably impatient group of tourists was forming, sighing and tutting at the silly woman blocking the wall. Legs shaking, I picked up the pace, looking like a big squatting bird on the charge. Reaching the safety of the tower, I apologised profusely and flapped weakly down the stairs to safety.

'And where was my family?' you ask. My family was gone. They deserted me, skirting back around the long way and down the stairs. By the time I reached the tower, they were down below, sampling the famous Brunello wine from the Montalcino area and purchasing snacks.

With Humpty Dumpty safely off the wall, the kids promptly chastened me for apparently always causing trouble or being embarrassing. Who? Me?

But there was no time to lose as we hastily drove the short distance to the 9th-century Sant'Antimo Abbey. In the heart of this beautiful Tuscan region, the abbey sits in a valley surrounded by peaceful hills, cypresses and vineyards. At certain times of the day, this beautiful Romanesque place serves as a background to the magical Gregorian chants of a small order of monks. They were due to begin in a few minutes.

As we approached the travertine stone abbey, the bells were chiming. We silently stepped through the stone-arched entrance with a small handful of other tourists and quietly took a seat on the worn wooden benches. The interior was shadowy and cool. The creamy alabaster carved columns supported vast wooden roof beams, crisscrossing high overhead. A carved statue of Jesus on the cross was positioned at the nave, surrounded by flickering candles casting shadows across the pale-travertine stone arches.

Bells chimed as the white-robed monks filed silently into the church, positioning themselves around the altar. They opened with a prayer uttered in Italian before the Gregorian chanting began, the enormous scale of the building providing exquisite acoustics. The hairs on the back of my neck and arms stood up. The monks' soft, lilting voices rose and fell in harmony, echoing mysteriously around the abbey. The words created a haunting, eerie melody softly floating in the air and around the spellbound audience. Candle smoke and incense wafted through the place.

Once the service was complete, we stepped out into the bright light of the garden. Bees buzzed and hummed through the lavender and rosemary. Cicadas rasped in the warm, rose-scented air. A white cat stretched and moved to the shade of an olive tree. The abbey garden held the same peaceful and calm atmosphere as inside the monastery, an enchanting place.

Later while I put washing on and started dinner, Geoffrey and the kids went out for a post-siesta stroll along with the rest of the village inhabitants. Every evening at the same time, a constant parade of people wandered by, heading for the main square. Well, everyone except The Munsters upstairs; we'd never seen them go anywhere except onto their balcony to stare at us.

Don returned full of excitement after calling in at the leather shop again. He'd sat down with an elderly Italian man called Giovanni, a leather designer and craftsman who had drawn a design for an inexpensive iPod cover for Don, allowing him to choose his leather and colour. Giovanni had a sore leg and had to go to the hospital in Florence the next day but promised to do his best to finish the project for Don before we left. Don was ecstatic about this. He and Jan promptly held another leather meeting.

It's funny what kids find to do without internet or TV. It was a pleasure to see them actually talking to each other for a change. And I knew when we left Tuscany and listed our favourite things, Geoffrey and I would name cultural attractions and those kids would say 'the leather shops and the butcher's'. Who'd have thought?

The following day we had a quiet time exploring a couple of nearby villages and generally cleaning the villa, ready to depart the next day. After a siesta we joined the villagers for the *passeggiata*, the social event of the day. It's rumoured that occasionally you may even get to see a family of 'French idiots' making a spectacle of themselves.

The elderly residents can usually be spotted sitting companionably along benches, observing life and sharing their day with each other. Stop for a gelato, drink or appetiser as you wind your way through the streets. Or if in Panzano, head to the butcher's shop, where we found ourselves for Friday festivities.

You wouldn't normally associate a butcher's with Friday-night carousing, drinks, nibbles, blaring music and village gossip. We were by now familiar faces to the locals of Panzano, even if we were known as 'those French idiots'. Dario's assistant plied us with red wine and snacks. The floor vibrated to the thumping sound of Bon Jovi's 'Livin' on a Prayer' accompanied by intermittent THWACKS from Dario smashing through a meat joint. Jan and Don stood grinning. Dario decided what we must have for dinner and cut us off thick slices of pork roast rolled in herbs, with crackling and a jar of red-pepper jelly.

As we staggered back home, merrily clutching our pork and full of joie-de-vivre, The Munsters stepped out onto their balcony.

'*Au revoir, messieurs,*' I sang out, cheerfully waving.

'What are you doing? We're not in France,' whispered Geoffrey.

'Well, everyone thinks we're French, so why not?' Either way, there was no response from above.

The pork was flavoursome and so tender it melted in the mouth. The herb crust tasted of summer.

After dinner, Geoffrey and Don strolled back down the road to the leather shop to visit Giovanni and Simona to see if Don's iPod cover was ready. Jan and I were packing. The next day we were leaving Tuscany and heading back to the Amalfi Coast to spend two weeks at a holiday rental in Massa Lubrense.

The boys finally reappeared after an extended absence, Don unusually animated with excitement.

'Guess what, Mum?' he blurted. 'They've decided to create a line in iPod covers, all because of me,' he announced proudly. I sensed another stimulating leather meeting coming on.

'I asked Simona about our upstairs neighbours,' reported Geoffrey.

'Oh yes. What did she say?' I asked, keen to hear this little snippet.

'Not right in the head,' he declared.

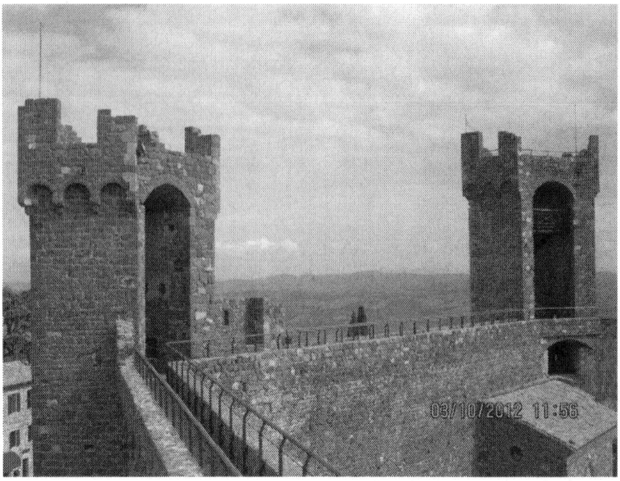
03/10/2012 11:56

GROTTO, GUNS AND GYPSIES

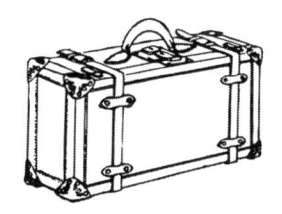

'Jeez,' yelled Geoffrey.

'Proceed straight for 500 metres,' commanded Marjorie the satnav.

Angry locals blocked our path, frantically waving their arms and pointing back the way we'd come. An elderly lady hung out of her balcony window above us, pegging out her washing and watching with interest. Nothing much usually happened along her narrow cobblestoned lane in Castellammare. Geoffrey sucked in his cheeks, sweating profusely as he was forced to execute a 27-point turn thanks to the reckless demands issued by Marjorie, sending us down a one-way alley. We retreated apologetically.

It appeared we were in the hands of a psychotic satnav with a death wish. All we wanted to do was get to Massa Lubrense in one piece. Geoffrey let loose a volley of expletives at the mad Italians coming at us from all directions at the next intersection. The kids giggled in the back seat; their father's outbursts helped pass the time.

'Look at that!' exclaimed Jan.

'What?' I asked.

'We're in a town called Angri, just like Dad,' she spluttered. Everyone laughed, including poor Geoffrey.

Sure enough, ahead of us was a big board pronouncing to all who passed it that we were about to enter Angri town. This wasn't good news; we weren't meant to be anywhere near there. We were still lost.

So we were understandably frazzled when we finally arrived in the little square of San Francesco in Massa Lubrense. Here we were to meet the house manager, Laura. But no one was about, and I mean no one. I looked around for the house, somewhat puzzled by the lack of any homes within sight. I could see a pizzeria, a church and an empty car park; something didn't add up. Geoffrey unclenched his grip on both the steering wheel and his jaw, his shoulders slumping in relief. We got out of the car, stretched our legs and waited. I was beginning to wonder if I'd managed to get us into another pickle of some sort.

A beat-up Fiat hatchback covered in mud rolled to a stop beside us. A scruffy young man with jeans hanging halfway down his bum got out of the car, fag hanging out of his mouth, raised the boot lid and told us to give him our luggage.

Seriously? I thought while glaring at him. *He thinks we're just going to hand over all our goods? He doesn't even have a weapon. I reckon I could take him out myself! Is this some sort of pre-arranged holdup: arrange to meet the tourists in a secluded spot then rob them?*

Geoffrey's cogs were still turning, wondering what to do, when a second but smarter car pulled up and out hopped Laura.

'Oh, I see you've met the house owner's son. He'll transport your luggage; we'll walk,' she said. Laura explained that we couldn't take our car as there wasn't a road but a narrow terrace cut into the side of a hill.

Oh, so that's what was going on. I relaxed. *But where the heck is the house? This wasn't mentioned in the brochure.* Fag End, the son, was roughly tossing our bags into the small boot of his tiny hatchback. It was like trying to fit an elephant into a shoebox. He gave up and drove off with the boot up, bags bouncing, speeding off down a narrow dirt path, ciggie smoke billowing from the open window.

Laura set off after him on foot. Grabbing our smaller bags on wheels, we hastened after her, dragging them through dirt and squashed olives that had fallen from the grove on the terrace above.

Before we were even halfway to the house, Fag End came careening back down the path towards us, forcing us to flatten ourselves against the wall while he passed, fag still clenched firmly between his teeth, smoke puffing out of the window.

Eventually a sunny, two-storey white house came into view, facing the view over Massa Lubrense below. *Excellent, I did OK here*, I thought, relief washing over me. That was before Laura led us down a path around the back of the house to a basement apartment dug into the side of the sloping land. It was almost subterranean, the view over Massa Lubrense gone. Inside, the apartment was modern, tiled and spacious with just one row of windows that looked out onto a tiled patio, complete with a gazebo and in-ground pool. The bedrooms and bathroom were set back in the basement, windowless and dark. But that was OK; who could complain with that beautiful patio and pool? We would certainly make good use of them. Thick, overgrown vegetation, groves of olives and fragrant lemons surrounded the apartment.

We walked back along the track to the pizzeria at sunset, pausing to watch the cheerful wee bats swooping and diving, expertly catching insects on the fly. Brightly coloured fairy lights lit up the pizzeria, looking enchanting in the otherwise deserted square. We were relieved to see our car was still safely in the car park, complete with all four wheels.

Once we were seated on the balcony under the lights, the waiter took our pizza and drinks order. Our Italian mysteriously failed again and an entire carafe of red wine arrived instead of a glass. Geoffrey gallantly helped to swig down the strong plonk, soon forgetting all about his stressful day at the hands of Marjorie the satnav.

BOOM! A deafening blast rang out early the following morning. Bolting upright in bed, I glanced at my watch; it was 7 a.m. Geoffrey sat up, looking groggy and alarmed. A series of loud explosions followed. Peeping through the curtains, I spotted the neighbour, weapon drawn, striding through his groves looking for enemy birds coming to peck at his olives. Geoffrey groaned but couldn't get back to sleep under the constant volley of shots echoing around the house.

With everyone now forced awake, we got up for breakfast. A bleary-eyed Geoffrey urgently sought strong coffee. Afterwards, peace appeared to have been restored and all was quiet. Excited to have our own beautiful pool and patio, we eagerly changed and went out to make the most of them. Geoffrey dived into the pool first, resurfaced and raced for the side.

'Holy shit, it's freezing,' he shouted.

Don felt the water and retreated while Jan and I searched for a slither of sun in which to position the sunbeds. This was our introduction to a surprising feature of the apartment not highlighted in the brochure. In October our apartment, pool and patio were in the shade 24 hours a day.

BANG! Another gunshot rent the air, causing us all to jump. This was followed by piercing squawks from an indignant bird. Another volley rang out and a bird fell from the sky. Loud crackling sounds came from just over the fence; flames licked at the air and smoke puffed gently around our patio, enveloping us in a smoky cloud. It was autumn in rural Italy and the season to burn the grapevine trimmings. Time to retreat indoors.

BANG! Another shot rang out.

'Oh flippin' heck,' blurted Geoffrey. 'Another great rental you've chosen. Let's go out then.'

We could only laugh. The neighbours were just going about their business. Life doesn't stop because pesky tourists arrive off-season. Escaping the smoke, gunshots and falling birds, we decided to head along the Amalfi Coast to visit the Emerald Grotto in the charming bay of Conca dei Marini. The grotto is a partially submerged cave where the sun shining through the cave entrance gives the water within a deep emerald appearance.

Here we climbed aboard a flat-bottomed wooden row boat after paying €5 each, thinking we were off to explore the cave with our masterful rower. The joke was on us as what we could see at the entrance before stepping on board was everything there was to see. Our Italian rower untied the rope and we set off on our cave exploration, went a few strokes, turned and circled back to where we'd just hopped on. We glanced at each other and grinned. The circling of this small area continued just long enough for the rower to turn on a portable ghetto blaster to play 'That's Amore' while serenading us about the moon hitting our eye like a pizza pie as he rowed around in what amounted to a big bath tub.

Oh, but let's not forget the highlight. We paused to look down beneath the surface at a tacky, ceramic Jesus covered in algae placed under the water. We gazed at it with about as much interest as we'd watch a blade of grass grow.

'You gotta tip *grande* for the sweet Jesus,' the man roared.

We looked at him as if he was out of his mind, unconvinced. So he responded by slapping the water from side to side with his oars.

'Looka, I make-a the water move for you; iss just like-a the Jesus,' he boomed. 'You gonna pay bigger tips for thees.'

He's out of his mind.

But in some twisted way, we loved it for all the wrong reasons. It was so bad that it was good. In fact I would do it again just for the laughs. And did we give him a tip? Well, considering he stood barring our way off the boat with his big, outstretched hand in front of our faces, yes we did. The implication was clear: you pay or I knocka you in the water.

Next day we set off to view the archaeological park of Herculaneum in the town of Ercolano. Driving there we wisely took the paid *autostrada* route to avoid getting lost. As Geoffrey pulled into the tollbooth, a swarthy-looking gypsy woman suddenly appeared, stepping out from behind the unmanned tollbooth. She stood in front of the payment machine and coin slot.

'It's broken. Ten euros,' she demanded, hand out quick as a rattlesnake.

A frowning Geoffrey hesitantly passed her a €10 note.

'It's a scam,' I whispered to him.

But it was too late; she'd caught us off guard. She turned and with her back to us, we heard the unmistakable sound of a coin clinking into the slot. The barrier arm went up. We needed to drive through before the barrier lowered again, driving off minus our money and self-respect. Mrs Gypsy pocketed our €10 note and Marjorie the satnav quietly sniggered and called us fools.

Tourists have distinctly different licence plates in Europe depending on their car's country of origin. We were clearly the French idiots. This made it easy for the gypsies just to pop out when they spied the next tourist target approaching. Thinking back, we realised we'd travelled on this particular section a couple of times previously and been charged a set fee of €2 at the automated tollbooth. Geoffrey was highly irritated at being so naively and easily duped.

'I hope she's there on our way back,' he grumbled.

'Why, Dad? What are you going to do?' asked Don.

'I don't know yet,' he replied, 'but she sure ain't getting another ten euros out of me.'

Herculaneum, a town similar to Pompeii but smaller, had also been buried by the eruption of Mount Vesuvius. As it was smaller, it was a simpler site to explore on foot. The artefacts were better preserved than Pompeii, creating a much greater visual impact. It was easier to imagine what life here must have been like in AD 79. Herculaneum had been a popular seaside town with the Roman elite, filled with grand villas. Walking around, absorbed in history, we felt as though we'd stepped back in time.

Later, on the way home, we stopped at our local corner store, aptly named Spendimeglio, to buy bug spray and mosquito repellent. A second, undisclosed natural feature of the apartment was a thriving colony of mosquitoes, drawn by the shady dampness and dense vegetation.

That evening the kids wrote postcards, read their books on Herculaneum and caught up on school work while I got dinner ready. Mosquitoes lay in various states of twitching death upon the white tiled floor, looking like chocolate sprinkles. After dinner we piled onto the big bed to watch a *Miranda* DVD on the laptop, accompanied by intermittent slapping of limbs and bursts of bug spray.

The next day, autumn made its presence felt. Heavy rain drummed down on the shiny, tiled patio, turning it slick. The track out to the car was filled with muddy puddles and squashed black olives. Shopping in Sorrento seemed a good plan, with the first purchase being umbrellas. But eventually the light rain turned into a downpour, sending us scuttling for shelter.

The kids steered us into a café and bar in the main square, chosen because of the all-important sign—free Wi-Fi. With the rain intensifying, it wasn't long before leaks filtered through the bar's gazebo roof. The canvas cover started to bulge, filling with heavy pockets of water, threatening to collapse inwards. Geoffrey and I sipped our coffees contentedly, legs outstretched above the water, new umbrellas held aloft. The kids had found the perfect Wi-Fi signal; we were going nowhere.

Early the next morning, we were again woken up by gunshots at dawn, courtesy of our bird-scaring neighbour. After a restless night spent spraying and scratching, I shoved the pillow over my head. At breakfast we admired the smoke billowing past our windows and laughed. I swept up the mosquito carcasses and sprayed more bug repellent. We were quickly adjusting to rural Italian life.

The day's plan was to head for Mount Vesuvius via the same *autostrada*. As we approached the tollbooths, the very same gypsy lady stepped out in front of us and demanded €10. Geoffrey was having none of it. Jan, Don and I stared at him, pondering what he might do.

'Get out of the way before I feed your teeth through the coin slot,' barked Geoffrey. The kids chortled in the back, surprised at their dad's rather clever humour.

He reached around the woman and shoved a €2 coin (not her teeth) in the slot; the barrier opened and we sped away. Marjorie the satnav applauded us for not being so stupid this time.

Driving up Mount Vesuvius, we found ourselves in a spectacular volcanic landscape of black-rippled lava flows, vents and fumaroles. Geoffrey and Don enthusiastically climbed the rest of the way to the crater. Jan and I felt no such need to exert ourselves climbing a mountain when we could clearly see it from the car park. We took the 'Vesuvius for the bone idle' option and browsed the car park vendor stalls for postcards while sipping on a cappuccino. After marvelling at the size and scale of Vesuvius, both kids wanted to go back to Herculaneum to finish exploring the ruins. The whole experience was even more meaningful to them now that they had the context of the volcano itself to apply.

That night Don and I lay on the bed to watch his *Dr Who* DVD on the laptop; fittingly it was the Pompeii episode. Sitting outside under the gazebo later, we watched the little bats flit around catching moths in the light next to the house. Church bells chimed a melody somewhere below and mosquitoes carried on their breeding in the vegetation. Geoffrey and I sat quietly, enjoying a glass of wine.

Opening Don's school journal, I gasped out loud. I read it to Geoffrey. 'And Dad told the gypsy lady to get out of the way or he would feed her teeth through the coin slot.'

2014

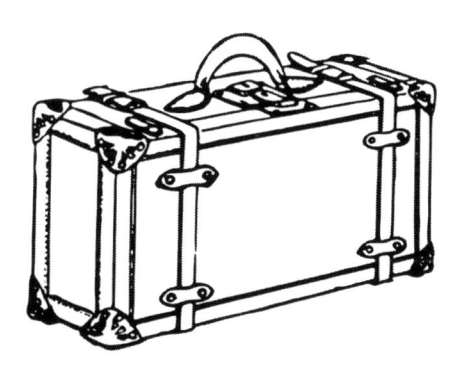

ITALY

WHEN BICYCLES GO BAD

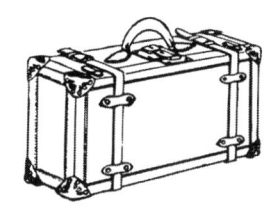

Two years later, in 2014, we went on one last trip around Europe together as a family. Jan was turning twenty-one and would soon be flying the nest. Don was fourteen and the following year he wouldn't be allowed to leave college for long periods due to exams. Our attitude was that if we waited until we could afford it, this opportunity would be gone and we couldn't wind the clock back. So we decided it was now or never; we were just going to do it, no time for regrets. A chat with the bank manager and we were off to Europe again for ten weeks. I wrote extensively about this trip in *Travels with Geoffrey*.

Over a coffee with my friend Louise, I broke the news to her that I'd just published a book about my family's funny travel mishaps. As a close follower of our daily travel blog at the time, the first thing out of her mouth was, 'Well I hope you included the bike-riding incident in Lucca. While I was reading your blog, I could just picture it all in my mind. I was in hysterics.'

'Oh shit,' I said. 'How could I have forgotten that?'

Who knows? Let's call it the menopause, but here it is, along with other excerpts from that week's journal and blog, especially for the lovely Louise.

A week's stay stretched before us in the seaside town of Levanto on Italy's Ligurian Coast, known as the Italian Riviera, about 60 kilometres south of Genoa. Our accommodation was a holiday house on a hill overlooking Levanto's long, sandy beach. The next day we would catch a train to the Cinque Terre (the Five Lands), a UNESCO World Heritage Site. Cinque Terre is a string of centuries-old seaside villages dating back to the 11th century. In each of the five villages, gaily painted fishermen's cottages cling to steep terraces surrounding tiny harbours filled with traditional fishing boats. Trains, boats and ancient walking paths connect the villages. Cars can only reach them with great difficulty from the outside, via narrow and precarious mountain roads.

Having dreamt of seeing this unique area for many years, I was filled with excitement. I was still recovering from tendon-repair surgery on my foot so couldn't do the walking trails connecting the villages, but I fully intended to make the most of the opportunity by exploring what we could in each little town. It would be a day to remember. And it was happening the following day. Ironically, in a Denise kind of twist of fate, guess what caused the injury to my foot? It was that little beggar Thomas the Tank Engine. I tripped over him at work so I suppose he got the last laugh there. There's probably a new Thomas book in the wings—*Thomas Does Denise*. Oh no. That doesn't sound quite right but you get the picture.

The following evening found me sitting outside on the tiled terrace writing in my diary, with Levanto's sweeping bay stretched out below me. The first lights started to come on around the town as daylight faded, the sun sinking on the horizon. Geoffrey was sprawled out on the bed resting; Jan was sorting through her photos and Don wandered in the garden. His interest in wildlife spotting hadn't changed over the years. Lizards were plentiful there, sunning themselves on warm tiles or rocks. We'd had a draining day which didn't go quite as expected. Let me tell you about it.

Having allowed plenty of time to get our train tickets that morning, we were in for a surprise. Upon entering the small train station in Levanto, we found it filled to capacity with tourists, but woefully understaffed. We looked around at the noisy chaos with dismay. Long lines of tourists queued at the only two ticket booths open. The oversized station clocks ticked loudly on the wall as we stood in line waiting.

Finally we were one person away from being served. My foot inched forward as the woman ahead of me completed her ticket purchase. But wait, what was she doing? Dithery lady was now choosing a T-shirt from the wall display, all the while droning on. Anxiously I glanced at the clock, shoulders tensing. The train was due in a few minutes. Behind dithery lady the queue of desperate passengers grumbled and groaned collectively.

The prominent vein in Geoffrey's forehead expanded, blood pressure rising. Dithery lady made her important T-shirt decision. I let my breath out slowly through puffed cheeks. From behind us, a man with a broad Aussie accent yelled out, 'Piss aaaff, lady. The rest of us are gonna miss the blaaddy train.'

Turning around she angrily scanned the queue for the perpetrator. No one exposed his identity. 'Rude,' she muttered before finally taking the hint and moving off.

Tickets in hand we raced to the validating machine to scan them before getting on the train. We had five minutes. There was a place to insert the ticket, a red light and three buttons. The instructions were in Italian. They might as well have been written in gobbledygook. In desperation Geoffrey started smacking the buttons as though playing Whac-A-Mole. Frankly a mole would have had more chance of validating a ticket than us. The Aussie bloke strode up. 'Jeez, mate, you're making hard yakka outta that.' Sighing, he took our tickets, swiped them and we were through. We ran for the train.

We found ourselves enveloped in a tide of tourists on the platform, all shoving their way onto an already overcrowded train which was very long but no match for the crowds. We squeezed in, sandwiched together like sardines in the hot morning air. *Well, hasn't this been pleasant?* Oh well, it could only improve from there for soon I would be enjoying the stunning Cinque Terre.

My cunning plan was to start at the farthest-away village and then work our way back along, hoping everyone else would get out at the first stop. They didn't. Apparently my plan wasn't so cunning. We all got out at the last stop—Riomaggiore. Alighting from the train, we were immediately swept along in a shoulder-to-shoulder conveyor belt of tourists squeezed through a tremendously long tunnel into the village.

Halfway along the tunnel, a busker with a piano accordion was singing the good ole tourist favourite 'That's Amore'. He was slightly off-key but a pleasant distraction from the smell of sweat. We continued shuffling along in a tight huddle of tourists towards the harbour. My visions of pastel-hued fishing cottages had been erased. Being short, all I could see of my surroundings were heads and limbs. Pungent body odours replaced the aromas of fresh sea air and delicate seafood dishes. It was rather underwhelming.

The small but perfectly formed waterfront was built for a handful of fishermen and villagers, not hundreds of tourists. It was difficult to move, let alone occupy a piece of ground long enough to enjoy any space or views. We needed caffeine desperately so we shuffled our way slowly back through the village, hot and miserable. The cafés were full. Instead of quaint, harbourside dining, we sat in a little fruit and grocery shop that also sold coffee. We were stuffed down the back of an aisle, next to toilet paper and sanitary products, at a cracked linoleum table. *This wasn't how it was supposed to look*, I thought, peering around me at the shelves of loo rolls. The picture I'd imagined was spectacularly different to this one.

Geoffrey and I drank our coffee in silence before we all traipsed back through the exceedingly long tunnel to get our train to the next village. The busker clearly only knew one song; he was still belting out 'That's Amore'.

We couldn't believe the crowd on the platform. Without shade, the sun was relentless. A lengthy, double-decker train pulled up but was already full. Doors started closing as people were still trying to shove their way on. We missed out by being too polite to jostle. Back through the tunnel of fun we went for a third time. The same, off-key song about a big pizza pie hitting our eyes accompanied our weary footsteps.

Lunchtime beckoned but choices were limited. The only place with tables free was naturally the most expensive restaurant in town. One look at the prices on the menu was enough for Geoffrey. He turned a sickly shade, grudgingly eating in silence before an excessive amount of euros passed through his reluctant hands. Our happy little quartet tramped back through the tunnel for the fourth time that day. Feet throbbing, we mooched past the piano accordion guy still belting out the same song.

'I'd like to shove a big fat pizza pie in his face,' grumbled Geoffrey quietly. Instead we shoved our way onto the next train by being ruthless like everyone else. My feet were knackered and I hadn't set one foot on any of the beautiful scenic paths the Cinque Terre is renowned for but just gone through one ridiculously long and stupid tunnel.

Our next stop was Manarola. This would be better. I felt it in my bones. We got out of the train full of hope then saw the subway tunnel. Inside, a backdrop of cracked tiles, graffiti and a distinct smell of urine set the ambience off nicely. I couldn't tell you what Manarola even looked like as we again did the squashed-sardine shuffle, feeling bad for the residents trying to go about their daily lives and that we'd contributed to the problem. There wasn't room to breathe so we left.

Vernazza was our last village for the day. Yes, there are five villages, but we just couldn't take any more. Upon alighting from the train, we were pleasantly surprised to find there was no long subway to walk, no stink of urine and BO, no more songs about pizza pies. The main village street winding down the hill towards the harbour was wider and dotted on either side with quaint little shops. We arrived at the waterfront and smiled. Vernazza was as pretty as a picture. The promenade was charming and more spread out so you could find a bit of space.

We purchased gelatos from a smiling young man at a sidewalk stand before meandering around the waterfront. From the farthest point of the marina, we stopped to sit and gaze back at the panorama. Colourful houses marched in rows down to the harbour's edge. They were met by a ring of equally colourful boats bobbing on glinting water. Vibrantly striped awnings and umbrellas lining the shore added to the rainbow effect. At the foot of all this colour, children and adults alike sunbathed on rocks or swam, watched by day-trippers licking an assortment of rainbow-hued gelatos. The sound of many languages mingled and drifted on the breeze.

It was difficult to leave this utopia but it was getting late. We reluctantly dragged ourselves away and ambled slowly back to the train station, looking in the little shops as we went. On our way back up into the village, another train disgorged a sea of tourists. We stepped aside into a doorway as they swept, tsunami-like, towards us. I sighed, relieved to have briefly found a corner of the Cinque Terre where we were able to appreciate its unique charm. Hopefully one day the local people can reclaim their most delightful villages.

Prior to leaving home on this trip, I'd trained for hours on my exercycle. In my mind I was practically a middle-aged Olympian. The reality was different but I was preparing for a challenge. I'd read online that you could bike around the historic, centuries-old walls of Lucca in Tuscany. They were built to protect the city and now provide expansive vistas for walkers and bike riders. *I'll do that*, I thought. *How hard can it be?*

But first I'd had to equip myself with some Olympic cyclist-type gear for the training sessions. My butt and other parts of my anatomy were getting sore on the hard exercycle saddle. Jan bravely accompanied her middle-aged, tubby mother into a specialist bike shop for elite athletes like me. I just wanted a padded or gel bike-seat cover to cushion the discomfort. We slunk around the shop trying to remain unseen while scanning the shelves but couldn't find what we were looking for. I was forced to ask the young male attendant. I kept my voice low while explaining about my sore nether regions, hoping not to draw attention. He said they didn't have any padded seat covers but he had just what I needed. The young man trotted off to find whatever it was.

He returned holding up some tight Lycra bike shorts with what can only be described as a nappy or diaper sewn into the bum, and some sort of braces to hold them up. Jan gasped in horror.

'Here you go, madam. If you try them on then pop out here, I'll check the fit for you.'

I heard giggling from somewhere behind me and a snigger from some fit young thing. The young man tried his hardest to persuade me to try on these fancy-pansy bike pants. Jan was doubled over laughing while I just stared at them in horror.

Finally I blurted out, 'Do you seriously think I'm going to come out here, wearing a nappy covered in skin-tight Lycra, held up by braces and parade about? You're out of your mind, young man.'

And with that, we scuttled out, red-faced. To this day I use two folded towels draped across the seat and I've never set foot in a bike shop again.

Well I did it. I actually did bike around the walls of Lucca, 4.2 kilometres on an actual moving bike, as opposed to my stationary exercycle.

To say my family had been dubious about my ability to ride a bike is putting it mildly. In fact they were pretty vocal with their derisive remarks, which only made me more determined. *I'll ride a flipping bike if it kills me.* After selecting our trusty steeds, I walked mine up the slope to the cycle walkway on top of the protective walls of Lucca. By then I just wanted to get the ride over with as quickly as possible before I lost my nerve.

Lycra-clad cyclists whizzed past us. My confidence deflated but I grinned at the memory of the nappy pants. Geoffrey, Jan and Don hopped on their bikes and watched me expectantly. *I'll show them*, I thought, attempting to launch myself. But the seat was too high; my feet couldn't reach the ground. I was forced to wobble precariously to a bench, grabbing hold of it clumsily. The kids were already in stitches but I was determined to prove to them that their mother could still ride a moving bike. Everyone else could do it. How hard could it be? I remembered that the last time I'd ridden a bike was 30 years earlier. You can't forget that sort of stuff, can you? In fact I was in a girl's cycle-racing team in high school but no one believes me. I only joined the team to chase the boys. Sadly they were too fast for me and got away.

Geoffrey lowered the seat for me. Well, technically he slammed it down impatiently as low as it would go. Adjustments made, I was ready for the second launch. But now the seat was too low. Every rotation of the pedals forced my poor knees up towards my chin. I wasn't designed for such flexibility. Geoffrey was called upon to make further adjustments, sighing heavily, while the kids made suitably unhelpful remarks. They were understandably getting impatient to set off. Finally the seat was sorted and I was ready for take-off. This time I had to stay on the bike.

In my defence, take-off wasn't helped by us being on a slight incline so it took three false starts before I was away. And when I say away, I mean careering out of control, screaming as I swerved off the track, completely forgetting that I needed to steer the thing. In retrospect I should have considered steering and braking before this very moment. On my exercycle the handlebars were just things to hold onto; they served no other purpose. So it was a momentary shock to realise I now had to steer with them. A few moments of wild weaving ensued until I gained some semblance of control.

The others had had enough of waiting for Mum. As far as they were concerned, I was good to go. Geoffrey and Don were already out of sight by the time I was able to glance ahead. I shouted out to Jan to ask where the brakes were. I didn't hear her reply and then she was too far ahead. All I remembered was that I used to stop my old school bike by pressing back on the pedals, but nothing was happening. Shit. There was no choice but to keep going. I couldn't slow down enough to even think about stopping safely.

Flipping heck. I gained a lot of speed on the downward slopes, hurtling along like a giant tubby missile, ringing my bell to warn people to get out of my way. I was terrified and exhilarated at the same time. Vistas of historic Lucca, majestic towers, churches and quaint architecture shot by in a blur. I saw nothing but the path ahead of me and the terrified, startled looks of those I almost skittled.

Up ahead I saw a group of teenagers walking, spread right across the track. They refused to move for Jan but she expertly manoeuvred off the track onto the bumpy turf to go around them. Hearing my frantic bell ringing, the group turned to look behind. At the sight of me hurtling towards them, their smug faces took on the appearance of deer in headlights as they scattered up the grassy bank.

Next in my sights was a group of elderly walkers all over the track.

'Bloody hell,' I muttered under my breath in alarm. Maiming the elderly wouldn't be a good look. Ringing my bell frantically didn't budge them and I couldn't stop. I screamed in panic, 'I can't stop; get out of my way.' That did it. They dodged to the side, startled faces staring after me. 'Sorry,' I called. I became aware of the wind whistling through my hair. How flipping fast was I going? Denise strikes again.

I have no idea what the view was like. I was solely focused on gripping the handlebars, steering and trying not to kill anyone. I reminded myself to breathe, just breathe. On one of the slightly uphill sections, my speed dropped. I was finally able to glance down long enough to locate and test a lever; it turned out to be the handbrake. Oh the relief.

Just as well I found the brake as I was envisioning having to beach myself deliberately on a bank like a walrus leaping onto an ice shelf. I was dreading the public humiliation of a crash landing. As it happened, I came in for a reasonably smooth one, in my opinion. My family were by then back at the starting point waiting for me. I hurtled right past them at speed, heading directly for the grass bank and a bench seat I could see. I grabbed it with one hand, stopped abruptly, jerked and tipped off, landing like an elephant felled by a tranquiliser dart. My legs were like jelly and my hands were sweaty with fear.

'That was great fun. We're going around again,' shouted the kids.

'Oh sod off,' I muttered to myself, falling onto the bench to recover my equilibrium. *Perhaps I'll stick to exercycles in future. It might be safer all round.*

2016

NEW ZEALAND

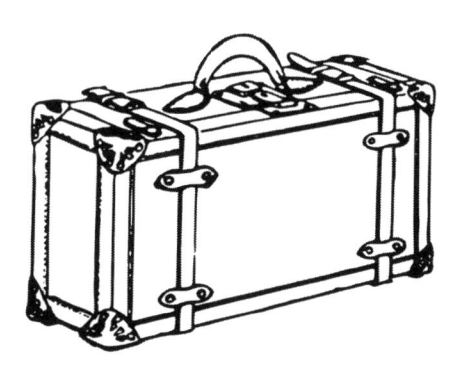

SAMMY THE SALMON'S SOUTH ISLAND SOJOURN

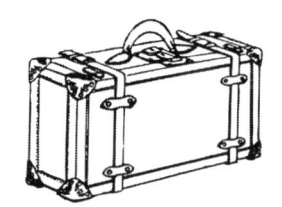

*H*ave you ever taken a salmon on a summer holiday? No? What about a rugby ball? I'm sure some of you will have taken one of those on holiday. But perhaps not carted a full-sized rugby ball around Europe for ten weeks just in case there was a need for it. Maybe we were keen rugby players, you wonder, which might explain this odd item taking up valuable luggage space. Umm, no. I have no idea why I took a rugby ball to Europe. It seemed like a good idea at the time.

But let me tell you about the time I took a salmon to visit all the most popular holiday spots in the South Island of New Zealand. It was the summer holidays in January 2016 and Jan was travelling in Southeast Asia so Geoffrey, Don and I went for a two-week holiday. I didn't pack a salmon, mind you. I acquired it on the first day.

We began our summer holiday in the legendary Mackenzie District, known for its clear starry skies, the highest mountains and the longest glacier in New Zealand, vivid turquoise lakes, golden grasslands and swathes of colourful lupines lining the shores of Lake Tekapo.

The skies were clear and blue, the sun heating the inside of our car. We stopped for lunch at High Country Salmon, a salmon farm near Lake Tekapo on our way to the holiday cottage we'd rented at Lake

Pukaki. The Chinook (or king) salmon are bred in the glacial waters of the Mackenzie Country hydro canal. Sitting outside on a deck built over the water, we ate lunch while watching the work going on around us. Every now and then, we heard a splash as a salmon leapt out of the water, creating circular ripples on the still surface.

With our tummies full, we bought a bag of salmon food to feed the leaping fish from the floating pontoon. As we were the only visitors that day, the salmon went into a feeding frenzy, lunging out of the water for all their worth, scales glinting in the sunlight.

'I want a salmon,' I announced.

'Don't be ridiculous, Mum,' said Don.

'I'm going to buy one,' I said and walked back into the shop.

Geoffrey and Don looked at each other, feeling uneasy. Surely I wasn't going to buy an actual fish?

Geoffrey called out in alarm, 'Where the heck do you think you're going to keep a blimmin' fish?'

Too late. I'd purchased one large Chinook salmon, its eyes glinting brightly as it was wrapped up. No, of course it wasn't a live one; it was dead. I was going to cook Sammy the salmon and he would be delicious. Geoffrey and Don were relieved to see the big fish wrapped in paper and breathed a sigh of relief—on with the holiday.

We carried on to the cottage on the shores of Lake Pukaki and unpacked. It was a fairly basic, old farmworkers' cottage, but the view! Oh my, the view. The cottage looked straight out over the pure turquoise glacial lake with the Ben Ohau Range as a backdrop. I unloaded the groceries and popped Sammy in the fridge, which is when I noticed there was no oven, just a microwave, damn. *Oh well, Sammy can enjoy a few days at Lake Pukaki then come with us to Queenstown. We'll eat him then.*

During the week, we headed to Mount Cook National Park. We were going to do the Blue Lakes and Tasman Glacier view walk, described as 40 minutes return with a gradual incline with rock steps. *I can do this*, I told myself. I was at the peak of prime fitness, round and menopausal, two buggered knees, and a foot held together by a rubber band, courtesy of Thomas the Tank Engine. But I did have a magnificent wooden walking stick from France.

I assembled my best summer mountain-walking attire and dressed in a luminous green and white striped cotton dress with leggings underneath, accompanied by brilliant pink shades and turquoise Keen walking sandals. Complete with my wooden walking pole, I was absolutely made for the mountains. Nothing could stop me. Geoffrey and Don eyed my ensemble with looks of horror but wisely kept their fashion thoughts to themselves.

We set off and drove about 40 kilometres along the edge of Lake Pukaki to Mount Cook village at the base of New Zealand's highest mountain, Aoraki. From there we followed 7.5 kilometres of unsealed, dusty road to the Tasman Glacier lookout car park. Surrounding us were some of the highest peaks in the rugged Southern Alps. After stepping out of the car, we found ourselves in alpine terrain: shingle scree underfoot, interspersed with alpine grasses and Mount Cook daisies growing in rocky, lichen-encrusted crevices.

This will be easy, I told myself. *It's only a twenty-minute walk to the lookout and twenty minutes back; piece of cake.* I'm not sure who this timing pertained to but it wasn't me. I failed to heed the clue here— lookout. A lookout implies that you have to climb *up* something in order to be able to look *down* on something else. We set off at a brisk pace for about 30 metres, with the metal tip of my stick going clip-clop, clip-clop in the gravel. It sounded like a horse was coming, which wasn't far off the truth.

Ahead of us loomed the glacier's moraine wall, a parallel ridge of debris deposited along the side of the glacier. *Ah shit*, I thought, looking up. So much for the stated gradual incline. Now it was all uphill on giant rock steps not designed for short people. I'm not much taller than your average leprechaun. For me to get up these enormous steps, I needed to use my wooden pole as a sort of vaulting-pole-cum-javelin. Each step took a lot more effort due to my stuffed, non-bendy knees. The sun beat down and my face turned a bright shade of crimson. Sweat poured off me like melting glaciers in an advanced state of global warming.

But that wasn't the worst thing. Instead it was the well-meaning people bounding down the stairs, gasping in horror at the state of me and giving me (a) sympathy and (b) encouragement or (c) telling me it wasn't much further and (d) offering medical assistance. *Well, that takes the biscuit. I know I'm breathing hard, as red as a beetroot and drenched in sweat, but I'm perfectly fine, thank you very much.* So I stopped every few steps to suck in oxygen while pretending to be ever so interested in the nearest piece of stupid lichen or blade of grass. I hoped this would deter any more well-wishers. I was silently cursing Geoffrey, who had bounded off, taking the water bottle with him.

'And where were Geoffrey and Don?' you ask. They'd galloped up to the top, where they were sitting contemplating the incredible panorama of icebergs floating on the glacier lake. Eventually, in a near state of collapse, I reached them and staggered to the nearest seat. Geoffrey saw me and came over, asking, 'You ready to go down?'

'I just got here,' I growled through gritted teeth. 'Waaaterrr,' I gasped.

'What?' he asked.

'Waaaterrr,' I repeated.

'Oh, water,' he registered and got the drink bottle out of his pack. 'Isn't it amazing?' he commented before wandering back to the rail.

Glugging the entire bottle of water, I looked around me. Yes, it was spectacular. I slowly moved my limbs into a semi-upright position before walking like a stiff-legged tin man over to the edge. Gazing out at the floury, silt-laden glacial lake below, I could see small icebergs drifting gently around in the water. At the far end, the delicate ice blue of the glacier face glinted in the sun. I took it all in and breathed deeply. The gentle breeze cooled my blazing cheeks and dried the sweat rivulets. I'd made it. I just had to get down again.

We dined on a very non-Sammy lunch back at the cottage before walking down the lupine-strewn track to the lake for a refreshing dip. Being a tad sunburnt from the morning's exertions, I was eagerly anticipating the cool lake water. With the rocky lake bed plummeting straight down to unseen depths, I strapped the boogie board to my wrist, stepped in and launched forward onto my tummy. My resounding screams rang out in the silent alpine air. A family of magpies took fright. I was possibly shouting something about 'ducks'. I'm sure you get the picture. 'Duck, duck, duuuccckkk.' My frozen lungs gasped as I frantically back-paddled with my arms like a cartoon character. Two short legs pedalled like Road Runner, desperately trying to find a grip on the bottom of the slimy lake bed. Staggering out, wobbly with hypothermic numbness, I then snatched my towel and marched back to the cottage to begin a staged reheating of my inner core.

Geoffrey and Don said not one word but I'm sure I saw the corner of Geoffrey's mouth twitching. They'd wisely decided to lie in the sun for a while before entering the bone-chilling glacial lake. They held off with their laughter until I was out of earshot. The magpies settled back in their tree now that all the shouting about 'ducks' had finished.

Tomorrow will be easier, I thought as we sat in the darkness on the grassy bank beside the lake. Hot drinks in hand, we gazed skywards at the renowned Mackenzie Country night sky, a sea of stars. Rabbits shyly observed us from a safe distance while munching on blades of dry grass.

The following day we were booked to go on an excursion from the Mount Cook Hermitage Hotel. A Land Rover would collect us and drive us to the base of the Tasman Glacier Lake where we would swap to an all-terrain, eight-wheel Argo buggy; it sounded like great fun. This would give us a thrilling ride along the Tasman Glacier Lake walk but without any walking necessary—just my sort of activity.

Early the next morning, we waited in the designated spot out the front of the iconic Hermitage Hotel used as a base for exploring the National Park. A big, safari-type Land Rover pulled up in front of us, driven by an actual Nepalese Sherpa called Tenzing. No, only joking. I can't remember his name but he was, indeed, a Nepalese Sherpa working in our mountains over the summer. He asked us to hop in while he put our day packs in the back. I felt a rising panic as I opened the front door. It was so high off the ground, I couldn't even get my foot onto the kickboard step.

Geoffrey and Don were already climbing into the back seat. The open rear door provided me with cover if I acted fast. I had a split second in which to act. Taking a leap, I threw myself chest down across the bucket seat, arms scrabbling to find the edge of the driver's seat on which to drag myself into the vehicle. My feet flailed around for something to push against for extra leverage. OK, yes, I was planking across this poor gentleman's seat. But that wasn't meant to happen.

Oh, please don't let the driver open his car door yet. The universe once again roared with laughter at Denise. *Oh shit.* Our Sherpa opened the door and went to leap in. Except my head was on the driver's seat and I was sprawled right across the front bench, scrabbling about like an overturned tortoise.

'Are you OK, madam?' he enquired.

Red-faced, I managed to squirm and turn myself over, using the steering wheel to sit up.

'Yes, perfectly fine. I dropped something.' I lied. Oh the shame.

Mr Sherpa started the vehicle and we bumped our way out along the unsealed Tasman Valley Road. I spent the rest of the journey worried about how I would ever manage to get back into the Land Rover for the return journey. Not only that, but I may have snapped the hand-hold piece off the ceiling; it was dangling to the left of my head. Hopefully he wouldn't notice. Running through different scenarios in my head, I just couldn't see how they would get me back in.

What if I can't even climb into the Argo? I was filled with angst at my failings. The gravel road ended and there before us was a bright-yellow, all-terrain vehicle; our Argo awaited. I was so relieved to find it was low to the ground. With minimal gymnastics I was able to climb into the back of it, sitting opposite Don on a bench seat. Geoffrey sat up front with Mr Sherpa. All set and we were off. As it happened, it wasn't getting on I needed to worry about. It was my boobs or, more to the point, being knocked out by flying knockers.

There wasn't a track, just boulders, lots of boulders. I now saw the reason for eight fat wheels as we bounced alarmingly up, down, over and around boulders. Don and I weren't really sitting on the benches. We found ourselves flying into the air and bouncing down with a resounding, whommmppphhh. Then up again. My boobs were slapping up and down, up and down as we clung on for dear life, trying not to be thrown overboard, pitched head first onto a rock. Nope, no seat belts here, folks. This was as intrepid as I was going to get.

Ahead was a gigantic boulder probably around the size of a two-storey house. 'Let's go for a look,' shouted Mr Sherpa and put the Argo into a spin before squealing off around that massive flipping rock at full speed. We drifted into a slide before skidding to a halt. I spat out a mouthful of dirt and dust, looking down at my outfit, now caked in dirt, and unclenched my white knuckles. Don grinned at me.

'Jeepers,' said Geoffrey.

'Fun, yes?' shouted Mr Sherpa through all the loose dust he'd stirred up.

He gunned the engine, floored it and performed a series of doughnuts around the mammoth rock as if he was purposely trying to fling three rag dolls out of his Argo. My sunglasses were now coated in debris. I could barely see a darn thing. Geoffrey was blinded by a layer of thick dust on his specs but couldn't risk letting go to wipe them. Don was still grinning.

Mr Sherpa hit the brakes and yelled at Don to follow him. 'Come on, young man. We climb this rock,' he called.

'Is he out of his mind, Geoffrey? Do something!' I exclaimed.

Geoffrey leapt out and followed them up the rock while I watched agape as the trio disappeared before reappearing a short while later atop the monolith.

'Flippin' heck,' I muttered, quickly snapping some photos before they climbed down.

And what did I think of all this adrenaline-rushing activity? you might ask. I was so scared witless that all I could do was laugh uncontrollably and try not to wet myself. I grinned and Don grinned back; we were having an absolute blast despite the pain of boob whiplash and eating dirt. It was awesome.

That was until we got back to the Land Rover. *Oh no*. Geoffrey and Tenzing took matters into their own hands, literally, shoving me from behind. All they achieved was that I once again flew head first into the Land Rover, albeit faster than my previous solo attempt. Job done, they slammed the door on me. I righted myself and we were off. I made a mental note to avoid high vehicles wherever possible.

Sadly the Argo ride ended a few months later. I'm not sure what happened. Perhaps Tenzing actually did manage to toss some passengers overboard?

So what was next on Sammy the salmon's adventures? He was delighted with a trip to Queenstown until I informed him we would be eating him there for sure. But once again we were thwarted by no cooking facilities except a microwave and we just didn't fancy cooking such a special fish in it. Mind you, he wasn't looking quite so special now; his eyes were dull and cloudy and he was starting to smell a little, shall we say, fishy. But I didn't like to insult him. So Sammy enjoyed the sights of Queenstown and Glenorchy. We visited the Ice Bar, where I was tempted to ask them to store Sammy for a bit as his head and tail were too long for our motel's icebox, hence his smelliness.

Sammy enjoyed some gold-panning at Arrowtown and loved the popular boat trip on Milford Sound, a must-do activity for any travelling salmon. Milford Sound is a fiord in pristine Fiordland National Park, known for its inky-dark waters, towering Mitre Peak, rainforests and waterfalls plunging down sheer sides.

Sadly each location failed to provide the elusive salmon-cooking facilities. But I wasn't about to ditch that fish. I'd become quite attached to him. Geoffrey and Don were getting a tad tetchy by now as they hadn't been able to have any ice cubes or ice cream. The mini freezer box was now Sammy's home.

Finally we reached our last destination, Lake Ohau Lodge. At dinner that night, we were seated in the fine dining room, waiting with anticipation for our menu of locally sourced produce, imagining venison or succulent lamb. How ironic then that the waitress proudly presented us with plates of Chinook salmon from the same High Country Salmon farm Sammy had come from. It felt like the universe was mocking me. Meanwhile poor Sammy languished alone in our room, body half hanging out of a tiny icebox. We couldn't cook him and we couldn't take him home. An entire day's drive in the hot sun just wouldn't do a shabby salmon any good.

So poor Sammy the salmon was left behind, another unwanted, impulse pet purchase, abandoned by his new owner. So much for pets are for life. He was a good fish. I left a note for the housekeeper about Sammy's fine Chinook heritage and breeding but indicated that she should eat him at her own risk as he was now a downtrodden, dodgy-smelling Chinook thanks to the poor care he'd received at the hands of these heathens.

KAIKŌURA QUAKE SERVED WITH KAHLUA

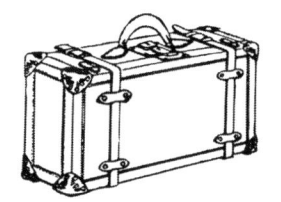

*L*ater that same year, in early spring, Jan was back home from her travels and working as a children's swimming instructor at the local pool. Don was fully occupied studying for upcoming end-of-year exams and Geoffrey and I were back to the grindstone, working hard to pay off the previous big trip.

November the 14th, 2016, is a day I won't ever forget. This chapter isn't about one of our holidays but what happened when Geoffrey's younger brother Gavin came to stay with us. He lives in Adelaide, South Australia, and periodically pops across the Tasman Sea to visit the family then often heads off on a good old New Zealand tramping trip, enjoying the Kiwi bush and mountains. Conveniently we live in the foothills of the Tararua Ranges north of Wellington, a good base for any keen walker. His trips are normally without incident; this time was different. He was like the bad-luck genie. Mind you, he always brings a plentiful supply of duty-free alcohol so his visit wasn't all bad.

Gavin arrived and parked his suitcase in our spare bedroom. Dark, foreboding clouds loomed. No, I'm not just being dramatic; they actually did. A damaging storm hit; the wind raged and the rain bucketed down, resulting in widespread flooding. Jan had a stressful drive home that evening from the pool, through flood waters and around a large landslip. We all gathered in the lounge except for Don who was studying in his bedroom for his exams.

'Cheers,' said Gavin, raising a glass of duty-free whisky to his lips.

POP. The power went out. Naturally we all blamed Gavin, who took it on the chin. We laughed, scrambling for the torch settings on our phones. A few seconds later, a beam of light entered the room. Don arrived in the lounge wearing his head torch. He spent the rest of the evening studying for his exams by tilting the beam of light onto the text. The rest of us chatted by the light of the fire, waiting for the power to come back on. It didn't. Outside, trees waved and bent; branches snapped and the wind howled on. We went to bed.

Power was restored by morning and the storm had eased. Gavin set off in a rental car to visit his sister, Stephanie. On the return journey, his rental car engine basically blew up on a remote country road. He rang to say he was stranded in a decidedly dodgy town, waiting for help. The car rental people were on their way to pick him up and fix or replace his vehicle. More importantly, he was going to be late for the roast lamb dinner I was cooking especially for him.

'Jeez, Gavin,' we said teasingly. 'What next? You're a jinx.' We didn't have long to wait.

The following evening all was well. We had no inkling of what was to come. We were in bed asleep at midnight, Jan and Don in their rooms at the end of a long hallway, and Gavin in the spare room down the same end of the house as them. Well, I say asleep, but for some reason, I couldn't nod off; perhaps I was plotting how to get that jinx out of my house before he caused real damage.

Too late. I heard an ominous and deep rumbling sound

approaching. I immediately knew what it was—EARTHQUAKE. Instantly alert, heart pounding, I sat up in bed. The ground started to sway. It seemed pretty gentle at first but didn't stop. After leaping up, I flicked the light on and grabbed my dressing gown, shouting out, 'EARTHQUAKE,' to wake Geoffrey. As I slipped the gown on, the swaying turned into violent, heaving shudders.

'What earthquake?' mumbled Geoffrey, still half asleep.

'THAT earthquake,' I shouted, without needing to.

Snatching a torch, I staggered across the moving floor to the doorway, finding it difficult to stay upright. Geoffrey was up in an instant, rushing to stand in the door frame next to me in the entrance room. We hung on tight. The dogs bolted in terror. Our cat shot past my feet, fleeing the house via the cat flap. The noise was deafening as the ground beneath me seemed to be trying to knock us off our feet. Far beneath us, the earth's crust groaned as it splintered and shifted. There were more immediate sounds of doors banging and swinging violently. Light fittings swayed. Photo frames on shelves fell; a mirror smashed. Pictures on walls drummed rhythmically against the moving walls. The dogs howled.

The lights flicked off during the most violent of thrusts. Everything went black. The world had gone crazy. An unseen enemy was shaking our house. The lights flicked on again then off. Seconds later they returned. The movement was subsiding. I felt sick and dizzy, my head unbalanced. The noise petered out. There was still a gentle, rocking motion. The wooden house frame creaked quietly as the movement dwindled. The pendant lights swayed eerily, casting moving shadows, but we could safely move again.

Geoffrey quickly grabbed a torch in case the lights went off again. Flying down the hallway, I stepped over a smashed picture, passing Gavin standing looking shell-shocked in his doorway, still holding the door frame for support. Pyjama clad, he stepped back into his room to grab a sweatshirt. Jan and Don came running from their end of the house, both talking at once. Panting, frightened dogs were getting under everyone's feet, seeking reassurance.

Everyone assembled in the lounge for a crisis meeting. Accusatory fingers were pointed squarely at our bad-luck genie, Gavin. Geoffrey put the jug on to boil while Gavin, Don, Jan and the dogs all set up camp in the lounge under blankets, keeping warm. With the fire stoked and the radio news on, they scrambled to check their phones, two questions on their minds: how big was that earthquake and where was it centred? Aftershocks rumbled on, unnerving us all further.

Phone in hand, still shocked, I talked to Nana and Poppa, checking they were OK. Their house was twenty minutes' drive from us in a tsunami-impact zone at the beach. I implored them to get in their car and drive up to our house, or anywhere, as long as it was inland and away from the coast. Kiwis all know the rule; it's drummed into us all the time: if it's long and strong, get gone. They were stoic or foolhardy in the face of adversity and refused to leave; they would stay in their house, assuring me they were shaken but fine.

We checked in with my sister, Helen, nephew and niece on the South Island. News reports were now trickling in that it was a 7.8-magnitude quake centred near Kaikōura. We later found out it had caused the simultaneous rupture along a long stretch of fault lines stretching up towards Wellington near us. Emergency services and civil defence were scrambling. A tsunami warning was put out for the Kaikōura Coast, North Canterbury, Wellington and the Kapiti Coast where we live. Helen and her husband grabbed a few things and drove inland as they live in a seaside village along the North Canterbury coast. We kept in touch with them over the next few hours as best we could, with cell-phone coverage dropping in and out, overloaded by the surge in demand.

I again rang Nana and Poppa, urging them to come up to our house in the hills which is built on solid ground, producing less shaking than their home built on sand. They'd seen the updated tsunami warnings and reports that a tsunami had been triggered. In Lower Hutt, over the hills from us, tsunami sirens were wailing as a trail of cars snaked up the Wainuiomata Hill, heading for higher ground. Eyewitness accounts were coming in of the water in Wellington harbour receding slightly and producing unusual currents. My parents decided it was time to flee.

Meanwhile news of the quake had hit news broadcasts worldwide on the BBC and American television stations. Australia is a couple of hours behind New Zealand time so Gavin rang home to let his family know he was OK but that we held him squarely responsible for this latest catastrophe.

I dispensed hot chocolate and biscuits along with shots of duty-free Kahlua from Gavin. It was for the shock, you understand—medicinal purposes. The kids were cuddling a dog each as we sat in shock, listening to the radio news of events unfolding. The world as we knew it changed that night. We had a new awareness of being powerless against a greater force; that in a fleeting moment, everything could change. As we listened and checked our phones, we all watched the creepy swaying of the pendant lights with each aftershock. I was talking to Helen on the phone when she suddenly paused during a particularly large aftershock. About 30 seconds later, it reached us after sweeping from North Canterbury across Marlborough, over the Cook Strait and up the Kapiti Coast. Jan pointed out the water in her glass sloshing from side to side. We appeared to be in a state of perpetual motion with an almost constant swaying sensation as if we were at sea on a gently moving boat; if only.

Our cat finally reappeared, wanting pats. Around 1:30 a.m., Nana and Poppa arrived to join our strange little quake party in the lounge. Hot drinks with a dash of Kahlua were dished out to the fresh arrivals and gratefully received. We made room for my parents on the big leather couches, along with blankets for extra warmth. The fire was stoked and glowing. There was comfort there in the room that night, comfort in the closeness of others, in the closeness of family. We had what mattered. We were together, bonded by our shared experience and our shared goal—get rid of Gavin.

With everyone settled, Gavin explained how events had unfolded down their end of the house.

'What woke me up was Jan yelling at Don to get under his doorway, before I even knew there was an earthquake. I leapt under my doorway to hang on, and even over the top of all the noise from the quake, I could still hear her bellowing, "Don, get up right now. I'm gonna smack you one in a minute,"' relayed Gavin. 'You must have been really worried about him,' he said to her.

'I wasn't,' retorted Jan. 'He's just a dim-wit. What were you even doing, Don? Why didn't you stand in your door frame like you're supposed to?' she demanded, glaring at her brother.

'I stayed in my bed,' Don casually replied with an infuriating level of disinterest.

'Well you aren't meant to.'

'Yes I am,' he retorted. 'You ask Mum. My bed is the safest place,' he announced. 'I can't stand below my doorway because my big French shield hangs above it. How would you like that to land on your head? Anyway, Mum's doing it all wrong 'cos you're meant to "drop, cover, hold" now, not stand under the doorway.'

'Well, you try dropping to the ground with my knees!' I exclaimed.

He was right. I'd lectured him often enough that he would have to stay in bed in the event of an earthquake because Geoffrey had hung that stupid weapon above his door frame. It was just waiting to knock him into the middle of next week if it fell. The rest of his furniture was pinned by hinges to the walls so the bed was his safest spot. Metal braces hold any tall furniture in our house.

Video footage of terrible damage was coming through, as well as reports of two deaths and others unaccounted for in areas cut off by the many landslides. After another couple of hours, the tsunami warnings were lifted. There had been localised tsunami waves closest to the epicentre. Elsewhere the waves generated weren't big enough to inundate coastal areas. Helen and her husband were able to return to their home for what remained of the night. Nana and Poppa also decided to head back to try and get some sleep.

We reprimanded Gavin for causing mayhem and enquired when he might be leaving our shores. We didn't want to tempt any further disasters. Everyone crawled into their still-moving beds in the early hours and tried to get some rest. Sleep didn't come easy. We were pumped with a cocktail of adrenaline mixed with Kahlua and still on edge. Every movement, no matter how slight, held the possibility of something bigger. Fear was lurking at the edge of our thoughts, keeping sleep at bay. Except Geoffrey; he, as usual, lay down, opened his mouth wide and began snoring in an instant.

But what I remember most from this night, apart from the horror of the earthquake, is the tale of Jan calling for Don, a big sister looking out for her little brother and trying to keep him safe, for his own stupid sake. Then there was the comfort in companionship, closeness, hot drinks and Kahlua—sweet, strong, duty-free Kahlua. Without Gavin's presence we wouldn't have had the medicinal alcohol. So perhaps he wasn't so bad after all.

A couple of years later, he and his family stopped over in New Zealand. No sooner had they touched down and entered Auckland airport than we had another quake. I rest my case, your honour. For once Denise was not responsible.

Some facts on the Kaikōura earthquake for those of you who may be interested in such things:

Shortly after midnight at 12:02 a.m. on Monday the 14th November, 2016, the 7.8-magnitude Kaikōura earthquake rocked New Zealand. It was centred near the North Canterbury town of Culverden, at a depth of 15 kilometres. The quake produced the strongest ground shaking ever recorded for an earthquake in New Zealand. It ruptured along a distance of approximately 180 kilometres, along more than twenty faults (a world record and one of the most complex earthquakes ever studied). The rupture lasted nearly two minutes, with horizontal and vertical ground displacement of up to twelve metres.

The quake triggered the biggest, local-source tsunami recorded in New Zealand since 1947, killed two people and injured over six hundred, caused widespread landslides, demolished houses, ripped up roads and railways and destroyed vital utilities. Tsunami sirens wailed across the Wellington region and severe aftershocks rumbled throughout the night, creating an unnerving sense of powerlessness and vulnerability.

It was a harrowing night that will be remembered forever by those who experienced it. In the twelve months after the earthquake, there were over 20,000 aftershocks, which continue to this day with decreasing frequency.

2018

MONTENEGRO AND CROATIA

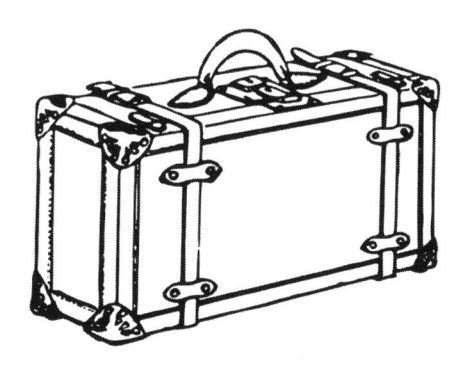

CAPTAIN JACK'S BALLS

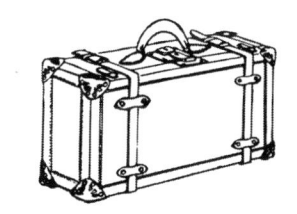

*G*eoffrey and I were travelling alone, venturing forth as new empty nesters. Jan was working in the Caribbean on a cruise ship and Don was in his first year at university in Wellington. I was a little sad to head off as a twosome, having treasured our adventures together as a family. There was one definite positive though: two people on holiday are a lot cheaper than four. I only hoped Geoffrey and I wouldn't get into too many scrapes on our own.

After beginning our journey with a few days in Venice, we drove our rental car, Cedric the Citroën, around the coast into Croatia. At the end of one particular day, we pulled up at Štacija Hotel on the Dalmatian Coast, overlooking the eastern shore of the Adriatic Sea. Once we'd checked in, we strolled along the shore, admiring the pale-sandstone buildings topped with terracotta roof tiles, a familiar characteristic of Croatia. A picture-perfect mirror image of each building softly floated on the glassy water; water so clear you could see each shade of stone on the bottom. Rising behind the hotel, forming a perfect backdrop, was a jagged range of karst-stone mountains in shades of blue-grey granite, typical of the Dalmatian Coast.

The friendly receptionist was genuinely delighted to have Kiwis staying and organised a table for us at their rooftop restaurant, seating us in a prime position overlooking the Adriatic Sea. A tiny paraffin lamp dimly lit each table, which could have been considered a romantic setting for two. The reality was two old farts struggling to read the menu without the aid of a spotlight and magnifying glass. Things quickly descended into our usual shenanigans.

The impressively suited waiter, looking dapper, delivered complimentary bread and an aperitif in a tiny cup to enjoy while perusing the menu. In the dim light, we presumed it to be a shot of fiery rakija, a common Croatian spirit usually served before a meal, so we glugged it back. Surprised, Geoffrey wrinkled his nose, holding the empty cup closer to the paraffin lamp, staring into it and sniffing suspiciously.

'That's not rakija. It's cold cucumber consommé,' I blurted quietly.

Looking around, we realised our faux pas. The other diners were using a teeny-tiny, delicate spoon to eat their cold soup, not glugging it back like peasants.

Turning our attention back to the Croatian menu, we resorted to switching our cell phones to torch mode to read it. We would need help; everything was written in Croatian. When our dapper waiter returned, we asked for his guidance. Geoffrey then ordered a steak with salad and I asked for the chicken with chips. The waiter looked confused and repeated, 'Chips?'

'Yes, chips please,' I replied.

He looked puzzled but nodded and headed back to the kitchen.

Our red wine arrived. Soon after, a second waiter in smart, black and white suited attire appeared by our table with a trolley. He proceeded to present my plate dramatically, lifting a silver dome to reveal an entire, enormous, fat chicken with a plastic bag of potato chippies nestled beside it on the plate. I stared at it, eyes wide, holding my breath in an effort to supress welling giggles until the waiter had gone.

Once he disappeared downstairs with the trolley, Geoffrey and I erupted into uncontrollable laughter, wiping tears from our cheeks.

Tucking into my scrumptious chook, I ate as much as I could before opening my bag of crisps. This was indeed a first.

The next day found us continuing our drive south towards Montenegro, with the mountains to our left and the iridescent, blue Adriatic Sea to our right. Wild Mediterranean plants, colourful oleander and herbs complemented the landscape. It was a lengthy but breathtakingly beautiful drive with many photo stops.

We arrived safely and settled into our apartment—a modern, crisp-white-tiled area on the second floor of a small development—in the village of Muo, overlooking the Bay of Kotor. From the picture windows and balcony, we could see cruise ships silently gliding past, entering the narrow harbour to dock alongside the town. Our apartment looked directly across the dark, inky water to the defensive stone walls of the Old Kotor Fort, built on the steep mountainside above the port.

Our first job of the day was to present ourselves to the tourist office within 24 hours. It's a legal requirement that tourists report there, telling them what you're doing in Montenegro, where you're staying and for how long. It sounded a little like communist Russia. Satisfying this demand meant heading into the old town amid the heat and chaos of thousands of cruise-ship passengers. We would have preferred to avoid it but the clock was ticking.

We found the tourist office inside the old town walls, duly queued and stepped forward at the appropriate time with a smile and a hello in the local language. The burly, uniformed official thrust his hand across the counter and barked, 'Passports,' without a smile or greeting in return. Taking our proffered documents, he snapped, 'Where stay?' Tentatively I held out a slip of paper with our address written on it. Grumpy-face snatched it off me, wrote down the details then demanded, 'Ten euros,' with an outstretched hand. I could almost hear his officious heels snapping together. He filled in our cards, which we needed to keep on us at all times, slammed them on the counter and we were done, dismissed. He waved us away with a flick of his hand. Nothing said 'welcome' like the Montenegrin tourist office.

'They can get stuffed,' I muttered on our way out of the door.

Job number two was supermarket shopping to stock up on food for the week. Stepping into the supermarket, we looked around in surprise. The place was dimly lit and there was an obvious scarcity of products on the shelves; even the freezers were largely bare. Our cooking options were going to be severely limited.

We parted ways to scout around. Eyes squinting in the gloomy light, I tried to scan unfamiliar labels for clues about the products' purpose. Not finding any cheese on the shelf, I tentatively asked at the deli counter, silently hoping they would understand me and my funny accent. The lady appeared to comprehend the word for cheese and passed me something closely resembling it. So feeling encouraged, I tried another avenue.

'Bacon,' I enquired.

She looked at me blankly.

'Bacon, pig,' I tried. No response. I had a lightbulb moment and let rip with a series of oinks, before looking at her expectantly. She glared at me, turned and stomped off. That was it, dismissed again. My humour was certainly lost there. At the checkout we smiled generously and carefully attempted to greet the staff using the local language. Not a word of response, not a nod and not a glimmer of a smile in return. I sighed.

If only they knew the effort those few words had taken us to learn. For me, travelling through multiple countries results in a confusion of languages all tied up in knots within my brain, being shot out randomly in a tangled mess. But I always give it a try.

After enjoying a meal of brick bread, rubber posing as cheese, and coffee with a dash of salt, topped with viscous lumps of sour yogurt, I suggested we live on cheap red wine. So there we were, Geoffrey and I, sitting out on our balcony with a glass of red wine each, enjoying our new diet. It was almost dark; the walls of the old fortress across the water were illuminated mysteriously; a boat disturbed the silence as it sped past. Crickets chirped; warm air languished motionless as I finished writing my journal, adjusting nicely to the new diet.

The following day we drove to Virpazar on the shores of Lake Skadar, the largest lake in the Balkan Peninsula. Interestingly the lake is half in Montenegro and half in Albania. Our drive there showcased Montenegrin driving as unpredictable and a little crazy. En route to Virpazar, we had the alarming experience of suddenly being plunged into completely unlit tunnels, nothing but blackness and thick exhaust fumes. We learnt to turn the headlights on quickly. But that wasn't the bad bit. Local drivers must have possessed some sort of nocturnal vision, suddenly appearing unlit from out of the gloom ahead, swerving to avoid us or passing from behind, unseen until the moment they drew alongside, frightening the heck out of us. Geoffrey's driving obviously registered as geriatric speed on the Montenegrin scale as we were tailgated the entire time by twitchy motorists in beat-up, dented cars.

So it was by pure luck that we were safely delivered to Virpazar, a tiny village, little more than a circle of stone houses, straddling the Crmnica River. This was the departure point for all boats leaving to tour the lake. The little hamlet sits at a fork in the river, separated by a historic, stone-arched bridge.

As we drove across the bridge, haphazardly parked cars lined both sides of the road. A busy street market bustled with stallholders shouting for business; tourists wandered aimlessly and boat-tour reps competed for custom. Geoffrey took one look then a deep breath, uttered his usual, 'Shit,' stopped the car and slowly reversed out again. We left Cedric on a dirt road before the entry bridge and walked back on foot.

Friendly reps immediately swamped us, inviting us to come on their various boat tours. With my knee issues, I wanted to scout out the boats first to see which ones someone with non-bendy knees could climb onto. I carefully studied pictures of the boats on posters attached to each little stall along the roadside.

I came to a stop; this one looked most acceptable. But perhaps I was paying closer attention to the captain instead of the suitability of the boat itself? OK, I admit it, that boat could have been a rusty tin can for all I cared. My chosen captain bore a resemblance to a certain Jack Sparrow: rugged, dark haired, deeply tanned, wearing a tight T-shirt and shorts that may or may not have revealed muscle-bound thighs. I wouldn't know as I didn't look.

My captain, Jack Sparrow, assured me his boat access wouldn't be a problem for my knees and promptly led me, ah, I mean us, down a riverside track to where the boats were moored. I would have followed him anywhere, quite frankly. The first issue presented itself. To climb aboard the vessel, I would need to jump across to the ladder. It was too far for me and I couldn't remember the last time I'd jumped anything. I hesitated, ready to back out.

'No problem,' assured Jack Sparrow, grabbing the huge boat and pulling it right up against the bank, muscles rippling in the sunlight.

'Thank you,' I crooned as I took his outstretched hand and climbed up the ladder before starting my graceful descent, step...step... 'Shit,' I gasped as I plummeted into space. The last step was about a two-foot drop to the bottom of the boat. I landed with a hell of a thud, like the sound of a cannon ball. He was lucky I didn't shoot straight through the floor of the boat. I stumbled forward, out of control, and landed on a bench, jarring my dodgy knees. Damn it. So much for trying to impress the captain. Sitting red-faced on the seat, rubbing my knees, I was filled with unease. How the heck was I going to clamber back out of the boat? More on that later.

So we set sail in our little wooden boat with a canvas sunshade, an outboard motor and our own Captain Jack sitting atop his captain's perch at the helm. To get to the lake, we had to putter our way down the Crmnica, a narrow, bulrush-enclosed tributary, leaving a gentle rolling wake unfurling behind us before entering Lake Skadar. The lake is one of the largest bird reserves in Europe, having 270 bird species, among which are some of the last pelicans in Europe as well as storks and herons, of which we saw none, not even a feather.

When the boat left the narrow tributary channel, the enormity of Lake Skadar unfolded before us with a sea of green waterlily pads as far as the eye could see, stretching across to vast, blue-grey mountain peaks enclosing the lake. Our boat puttered steadily out through narrow channels of clear water formed by the boats, bordered on either side by waterlilies. To our right an imposing, ancient stone fortress stood sentinel on the shore, standing guard as it had for centuries, its only inhabitants now being birds nesting among its crumbling ruins.

As I feasted on the sights, Captain Jack included, taking in all of this magnificence, my joyful mood was tempered by the ever-present thought that, somehow, I still had to climb out of this boat. Sitting staring at the huge step up from the bottom, I couldn't see how I was going to hoist my stubby little legs up that high. Yes, it was true; I'd got in, but only because I fell in, and last time I checked the laws of gravity, I didn't remember anything about being able to fall up.

I thought back to the humiliation of the Land Rover incident at Mount Cook. *This isn't a Denise problem. It's not my fault I'm short.* But on the other hand, the two stuffed knees were down to my own clumsiness. I injured one stepping over a chain-link fence. My foot caught it and dragged the whole fence out of the ground as I tumbled dramatically down a bank. Just to juice it up a bit, it was in front of the primary school at pickup time. I injured the other knee at work, simply answering the telephone; now that in itself takes a special sort of Denise-type skill.

Captain Jack Sparrow interrupted my thoughts in a spectacular fashion by offering me a traditional welcome gift of his balls on a plate. He'd handled these balls himself, moulded and shaped them in the privacy of his home, ready to present them. Homemade, battered balls with a shake of icing sugar on them, accompanied by a beautiful, homebrewed red wine. The sun was shining and I had Captain Jack's balls in my hands. Life was good. If only I could figure out how to get off the damn boat. I took a bite, mmm, a bit like a doughnut.

Captain Jack said we were the first Kiwi passengers he'd ever had on his boat. So with time to chat and balls to consume, I asked who the most annoying passengers were. He claimed Russians were number one, with the French a close second. Thankfully he was unaware of our history as 'the French idiots'. We tried to educate him on rugby but that got horribly lost in translation and involved further talk about different-shaped balls.

Despite the lack of bird life, dragonflies darted, frogs basked and the occasional fish disturbed the lake surface. According to the captain, the storks and pelicans were conveniently all down the Albanian end of the lake where we couldn't go. But it was a wonderful feeling, riding out on that glass-like lake, passing through acre upon acre of waterlilies, the lake silent apart from the steady putter of the engine. Perfection.

As we approached the end of the trip, drawing closer to Virpazar, I nervously asked if there was anything for me to stand on to reach that ginormous step. There wasn't. Captain Jack got on his phone and spoke in rapid Montenegrin. I didn't know what he was saying though I could imagine it went like this: 'Hi, I have a plump, crazy lady on board with the legs of a leprechaun. She says she can't get off my boat. Send help.'

As we approached the dock, Captain Sparrow pointed at a man and said, 'He will help.' There stood a man who looked like a Russian weightlifter, with a fag dangling from his mouth. *Oh my goodness. I'm not being manhandled by him.* One look at him and I was off, casting dignity aside. I leapt and did a half log roll onto my poor knees, grabbed the rail and was off that boat faster than a gazelle. Geoffrey was left in my wake, looking after me in astonishment—amazing what an adrenaline rush can achieve. I hadn't performed a manoeuvre like that since college PE class where we were forced to hurl ourselves over the wooden vault.

In a strange coincidence, I received a photo from Jan a few days later. She was standing draped all over a look-alike Captain Jack Sparrow on a palm-fringed, white-sand beach in the Caribbean. He was one of the cruise-ship characters dressed up to entertain the guests. Some people have all the luck. I chuckled to myself. *I damn near holed Captain Jack's boat!*

THE SMOKING GERMANS

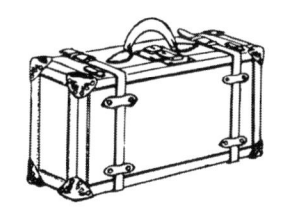

After leaving Montenegro we spent four days on the Croatian island of Korčula, where the bad-luck genie continued to follow us around. Our misfortunes included dental woes for Geoffrey, fleas, uninvited visitors, a storm and finally wildfires. However, there was one highlight.

I bravely stepped out of my comfort zone and booked us on a dune-buggy safari tour around Korčula, 25 kilometres of off-roading on dusty and stony tracks. I was 99% certain that I could actually climb into a dune buggy. Heading to the waterfront that morning to meet our guide, Ivan, we noticed a fire on the mainland opposite; it looked reasonably contained.

Our small party of tourists assembled: two older Croatian men in their early 60s, a party of six Germans and us. We greeted them and introductions were made, everyone smiling, excited about the day ahead. Ivan arrived, dark hair, thickset build with the look of a rugged outdoorsman, perhaps in his late 30s. He invited Geoffrey and me to sit up front with him; the others climbed into the back of the van for the drive to his family estate a few kilometres west of Korčula.

A row of stocky little dune buggies lined the roadside: four fat tyres, steel roll-bar cages and large, exposed shock absorbers. Choosing ours, we climbed in; finally a vehicle designed for a leprechaun. Our bums were only inches off the ground. It was disconcerting to see the road beneath me just in front of my toes; apart from a metal plate on the floor, everything was open. Seat belts on and we were ready for the full safety briefing. Ivan leant in and turned the noisy, single-cylinder engine on, pointed at a lever and said, 'Don't touch that,' followed by, 'You've got two pedals,' and that was us good to go.

The engines were all on, idling noisily, exhaust fumes hanging in the air. But we had to wait while one of the Germans, a young man in his 20s, had mummy carefully wrap a scarf in a turban around his head. They took their time. The other German men in their group got out of their buggies and stood around smoking as if they might never see a cigarette again. Ivan waited patiently. One of the Croatian guys in the buggy in front muttered, 'But of course ve must wait for zee Germans.' This was when we realised that perhaps all was not well in Croatian/German relations. Once the Germans were wrapped and fully smoked, we departed, with us at the rear.

With the single-cylinder engine revving like a straining lawnmower, we were off, at first on sealed roads as we made our way through town and onto off-road tracks. We rumbled and jiggled through vineyards, past ancient rock walls, aged olive trees, conical cypress and little villages, all with a backdrop of the bright-blue Adriatic Sea.

It was exhilarating. We bounced; we juddered and jarred; I whooped and laughed out loud, spitting out dust. We discovered too late the foolishness of being at the back as dust picked up from the dirt road flew towards us, a billowing, orange cloud. The others were leaving us in their dusty wake; we fell behind. Geoffrey gripped that steering wheel like he was Nigel Mansell, lent in and pumped that pedal for all it was worth. Zooming along in our roaring lawnmower, we bounced over rocks, flying along dirt tracks in the pine-covered hills above Korčula. Bouncing up and down in my seat, hair flying in a slip-stream, I laughed out loud.

Ivan led the group to the site of a World War II monument. Climbing out of our buggies, we stretched and followed him over to a fenced-off pit, high on the hillside. A plaque explained in Croatian the horrible significance of this site. Ivan informed us this was where the German Army had dumped the bodies of local Croatian people in their hundreds, viciously throwing them still alive down vast limestone caverns where they plummeted to their death.

Shit, this is awkward, I thought, looking around at the stony faces of the poor German tourists. Geoffrey stared at his feet, examining something imaginary on his shoes while waiting for the uncomfortable moment to pass. The two older Croatians fixed the Germans in a steely glare, not looking away, daring them to respond. Silence hung heavily in the air. The Germans broke the stand-off, turned their backs and moved away towards their buggies to recommence smoking.

'Bloody Germans,' one Croatian muttered to the other. Moving back towards the rest, Ivan picked a leaf off a bush as he brushed past it, calling out to ask if anyone in the group knew what it was.

'Sage,' I said instantly.

He looked astonished. 'Hey, New Zealand, last four years no one ever answer that correctly.' Denise for once was class favourite. For the rest of the trip, Ivan continued to pick samples from the vegetation and yell out, 'Hey, New Zealand, what's this one?' and I would look, sniff and tell him what it was. He roared with laughter every time and shook his head in astonishment. Denise remained firmly at the top of the class with a rapidly swelling head.

Once the young German was rewrapped by mama and the others had smoked some more, we set off again, with Geoffrey and me still bringing up the rear and struggling to keep up. I giggled and shrieked, sucking in the dust and dirt and loving every minute. Wind whipped my hair into flying tendrils. Perhaps I too needed mama to wrap my hair in a turban. Maybe if Geoffrey smoked a cigarette, we might fly like the Germans. As we drove through a village, some schoolboys on the side of the road all held their hands out to high-five the losers at the back as we sailed past. They cheered us on, or were they mocking us?

We stopped for what was going to be swimming time at the sandy beach of Pržina. But due to the wind, which had picked up considerably, we just had a coffee while the Germans smoked yet again. The Croatians, Geoffrey and I hopped back in our dune buggies at the appointed time, joined by Ivan, who peered at his watch. We all looked at the Germans expectantly. Young German was having mum rewrap his headscarf again and the others were casually smoking. By now I was getting irritated with them as well, not because of their nationality but just because they persisted in arrogantly keeping everyone else waiting at each and every stop.

'Of course we must wait for zee Germans,' moaned one of the Croatians. Poor Ivan paced; he had a schedule to stick to as he had another tour party booked for the afternoon. Eventually, with the Germans' lungs suitably inflated with smoke, we got underway and headed back to Ivan's family estate.

After a fabulous morning, we arrived back at the house where his mum, Ana, had put on a fine spread for us all from their property. She proudly presented their home-grown olive oil, red and white wine, bread, figs, nuts, cheese, doughnuts and fruit brandies then disappeared inside before bringing us all a tray of her homemade pancakes stuffed with figs. While the Germans busied themselves smoking a bit more, I charmed Ana by showing appreciation and attempting to thank her for the food, in Croatian. Geoffrey and I were promptly invited into the house, where we were led into the living room where Ivan's hunting trophies were proudly displayed. It turned out our host was one of Europe's most highly decorated hunters, and Ana was very proud.

We entered a room where all four walls were covered in skinned and stuffed bears, wolves, beaver, deer, fox, mountain goats and boars, as well as a hefty collection of medals and cups. Ivan had at one point been Europe's top trophy hunter and learnt his skills from his dad. He told us they hunt in the Dinaric Alps, a mountain range separating the Balkan Peninsula from the Adriatic Sea. These alps stretch all the way from Italy in the northwest down to Albania in the southeast. No matter our opinion on hunting—it's not something I would do—it was still an honour to be invited inside their family home and be shown this aspect of their private life.

From Ivan's family deck, we watched fire-fighting planes scooping up sea water to dump on the ever-increasing wildfire across the water. Smoke was starting to fill the horizon and we could now smell it. Ivan checked his phone, telling us the road was currently closed out of Orebić; the ferry to the mainland was stopped. This was concerning news as we were due to sail to Orebić the following morning.

Once we'd all finished eating, the Germans lit another quick ciggie just to get from the deck to the van. No, I'm not joking. It wasn't even funny anymore, just irritating. Ivan again ushered Geoffrey and me into the front of the van with him; the Croatian men hopped in the back and we waited once again. The Germans casually smoked their way slowly to the van before stubbing their ciggies out on the side of the road. As the last one climbed aboard, Ivan slammed the van door on them a little too hard.

When we returned to our villa, it was clear that the fire had got worse. With the wind intensifying into a gale, the army was called in. We could hear fire-fighting planes swooping low overhead at regular intervals. An entire village and all tourists had been evacuated over on the mainland across the water. We were supposed to be leaving the next day but were trapped until the road out reopened. Geoffrey headed to bed with toothache. Stuart, a stray cat we'd befriended, sat on the doorstep staring at me and meowing pitifully. Having spent a previous night convulsed with frenzied scratching after discovering he had fleas, I'd banished him from going near me. As I packed my bags, I couldn't help but wonder what would happen the next day and if we would get off the island.

Our villa owner updated us later that evening after speaking with her brother-in-law who also happened to be the fire commander. Things were serious, the worst wildfire in Croatia that year and rather unusual for this late in autumn. Geoffrey looked at me suspiciously and sighed, muttering something about Denise the bad luck genie.

THE BLACK CAT

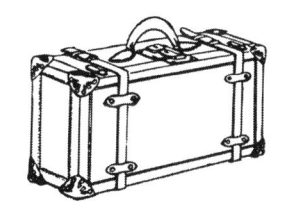

I found myself alone on a balcony at sunset, sipping a glass of wine and enjoying a Kit Kat while savouring the warmth of the last of the day's sun. The chirping of evening crickets surrounded me. I could hear the sound of shifting pebbles at the water's edge a few metres away and the dulcet tones of Geoffrey's snores coming from within the apartment. He'd gone to have a lie down, tired and stressed after our escape from the wildfires on the Pelješac Peninsula on the Dalmatian Coast.

I took a deep breath then exhaled slowly, thinking back over the journey. Early that morning, once the ferries resumed operating, we were on the first sailing departing from Korčula. The service had been suspended the previous day as flames surrounded the access road out of Orebić. On board the ferry, we found ourselves alongside many firefighters heading directly across the strait to the port town of Orebić to help their counterparts.

As we drove off the boat and out of Orebić, thick smoke temporarily enveloped our car, turning bright daylight into dull, ashen grey. Exhausted firefighters lay in groups under the shade of trees lining the road, grabbing a quick rest from the relentless task of battling the flames. Thankfully the wind fanning the embers had died down overnight, making their work a little easier. A Canadair firefighting plane roared past, swooping down low as it scooped up water from the sea on our right before banking steeply and turning back above the hillside on our left.

Geoffrey drove swiftly through the fire zone. Blackened, smoking trees and vegetation lined either side of the road right down to the water's edge. Embers periodically reignited, sending flames perilously close to our car. It was an unnerving experience and a tense journey; neither of us spoke. Smoke ahead of us on distant hills signalled another wildfire spreading across the Neretva Valley. The sight of a second Canadair plane swooping over the flames in the distance confirmed this.

With great relief we arrived safely at the tiny port of Drivenik where another car-ferry service delivered us the short distance across the water to the island of Hvar. At 68 kilometres long and only 10.5 kilometres wide, Hvar is like a long, slender finger off the Dalmatian Coast, its steep hillsides covered in pine forests, with vineyards, olive groves, fruit orchards and lavender fields dotted below.

We were staying with a local family in their upstairs apartment in Velika Stiniva, a little fishing village. After we'd turned off the main road at the tiny hamlet of Zastražišće, we wound our way down a partially paved, dusty road towards the sea. We drove through a flat, dry Mediterranean landscape before zigzagging downwards into a narrow, steep-sided gorge of limestone karst cliffs. The road then hugged the side of the gorge, eventually leading to the ocean and the little horseshoe-shaped beach of Velika Stiniva. Here the canyon ended in a small settlement of pretty stone houses dotted along each side. It appeared that every inch of the narrow, middle strip of land between the houses was being cultivated to grow olives, grapes, fruit and vegetables. Ahead, on the shore of the crystal-clear, turquoise bay, stood a tiny stone chapel, a little bar and a flotilla of gaily-coloured fishing boats.

After settling into our bright and modern little apartment, we joined the owner, Nika, for a glass of her homebrewed red wine and a plate of fresh figs. Nika was tall, slim, blonde-haired and younger than me, appearing weathered and brown from a lifetime spent outdoors. She explained that most of the families in the village were related; their ancestors were fishermen, boatbuilders and olive farmers. The village is largely empty for most of the year but comes alive over the summer months when families who emigrated abroad return, many from Australia and New Zealand. Nika described her life to us.

'I must work every day. Work, work, work. Much work to do. My husband, he goes out fishing and I look after our children. I take Marko now to feed chickens, then the cats, always work to do in the garden, planting, watering, picking, tending to the olives and vines. It is a hard life but a good life. Every summer our family visit from Australia. Ah, good times.' Nika paused and smiled. 'Then we play games, drink and party, work together in the fields and swim. My husband, he take family out fishing and barbecue fish for everyone to share. All the family get together to help harvest the olives and grapes. We work hard; we sing traditional songs and the old people tell stories. Yes, it is a good life.'

I sipped the last of my wine and slapped at my legs. The sun was setting and the mosquitoes were coming out. When I waved to an old lady working on the land in front of our apartment, she smiled and waved back as I turned and went inside.

It was our first full day at Velika Stiniva beach. Geoffrey was now refreshed and ready to explore. Things started off well. We opened our back door to head out for a walk and found Bob sitting on our doormat, scratching himself. Bob was brown and had shorter legs than me. He looked like a corgi. Introductions were made and we set forth for a wander around our little seaside spot, accompanied by our new friend Bob. He liked to take risks, it seemed, as he peed all over the sign saying 'No Dogs Allowed'. I liked his attitude. We called out '*dobar dan*' (good day) to the local fishermen who, in turn, looked at us like we were morons, but even that didn't dampen our enthusiasm.

We got underway in the car, heading for the ancient port town of Hvar. I inserted my Lukas Graham CD and began screeching out my own off-key rendition of '7 Years'. Geoffrey cringed in disgust. I was happy. Driving through the sparsely populated interior of the island, amid pine-clad mountains, we were offered occasional glimpses of the iridescent blue Adriatic Sea in the distance. All was right with the world. And then a black cat crossed the road in front of us. Didn't that mean bad luck in some parts of the world? I stopped singing.

'Oh shit, that can't be good,' said Geoffrey.

I made no comment. If anything bad happened this time, no one could blame it on Denise. It would be the black cat's fault.

But all was well. Good fortune rained down upon us. We found Hvar town without getting lost and even lucked a car parking space right by the centre. From there it was a short stroll to the impressive 16th-century St. Stephen's Square, sprawling over 4,500 square metres. The square was lined with cafés sporting matching white sunshades. The ancient cobblestones, worn smooth under centuries of feet, led us across a long, sun-baked piazza towards the emerald-green harbour. Here the water was so clear the boats appeared to be suspended mid-air. Impressive stone architecture in shades of honey lined the way, the most impressive of which was the 1605 Cathedral of St. Stephen, standing at the far end of the piazza with its majestic Renaissance bell tower.

We wandered happily, explored alleyways and had coffee at one of the crisp, sun-shaded cafés in the square. Still the gods shone on us. Next we drove up to the imposing 13th-century Venetian fortress above Hvar. From there the magnificent views took in the old town below, set in a picturesque natural bay with the pretty Pakleni island chain just off shore. These circular, pine-covered islands looked like a string of green emeralds from above. The palest blue of the sea and sky was perfectly offset by the green pines and red-tiled rooftops of Hvar below.

Because things were oddly going so well, we decided to visit Vunetovo Craft Beer Brewery that I'd read about online. The gods above had a little chuckle to themselves at our presumption that all was well. Had we forgotten the black cat? 'Fools,' they thought.

I had the address in my bag so we programmed Sassy the satnav and set off. Events turned sour pretty rapidly. Sassy started screeching at us to turn hard left, straight over a cliff. It's ironic that all our satnavs have a strange predilection for wanting to lure us over a cliff. Sassy wasn't happy when we ignored her; instead we followed the road straight ahead. She continued issuing orders.

'About turn.'

'Perform a U-turn.'

'Drive directly over the cliff. That is an order.'

Sassy little madam. Finally she went quiet. We thought she'd given up but she was secretly plotting her revenge.

A few minutes later, Sassy sprang back to life and appeared to be behaving lucidly and responsibly for a change instead of trying to kill us. So we mistakenly turned off and followed her directions. The road quickly tapered into a tight lane, becoming so narrow we had no choice but to continue. Opportunities to turn around were nil. Sassy had Cedric committed to a suicidal course. If a satnav could provide backchat, Sassy would be muttering, 'That'll teach them to disobey my instructions. Let them get outta this one alive.'

Sassy led us straight into a cave, a deep, dark cave. No, not a tunnel. It was literally a cave. But lo and behold, guess where the cave led us to? We landed on someone's rooftop terrace, a rooftop with a steep drop to the ocean below the house upon which we found ourselves perched. Looking around in alarm, I noticed the owner's sunbeds and potted geraniums. I didn't think this was a place for a dirty great Citroën to come to rest. People appeared on neighbouring roof terraces and balconies to stare at us aghast, no doubt wondering who these morons were, trying to park on their neighbour's roof of all places. This would seem to be a perfectly fair question.

Geoffrey told me off as apparently my screaming and flapping my arms about was a distraction as he tried to extract us off the rooftop and reverse out through the dark cave. My heart was beating fast and I couldn't help screaming as we inched back ever so close to the cave walls.

Once through, we still couldn't turn as that stupid Sassy had us tightly wedged where no car should ever have been. So it was a long, stressful journey in reverse, much like reversing out of a boa constrictor. We slowly edged all the way back up a steep hill, with Geoffrey cursing and perspiring and me switching between dead silence and hysteria.

'It was that bloody black cat,' blurted Geoffrey.

Happily extracted back to an actual road again, we got out of town quickly, abandoning all thoughts of craft breweries. Sassy was unceremoniously decommissioned. But we were no quitters. We decided to carry on to Malo Grablje, a centuries-old abandoned village situated a couple of kilometres inland from the bay of Milna. After turning off the main road, we headed along a dusty dirt road into a wooded valley carpeted with wild Mediterranean plants and gnarled, old olive trees. We found ourselves entering a steep-sided valley, remnants of ancient dry-stone wall terraces clinging to the slopes. Cedric bounced along the rutted way, leaving a reddish-brown trail billowing behind us.

The track came to a dead-end at the village. On our left, meandering up the wooded hillside, were the abandoned stone houses of Malo Grablje. We stepped out of the car to an eerie, still silence, the only sound the steady hum of cicadas in the humid air. As we walked, clouds of yellow and black butterflies fluttered around, disturbed by our movement. Malo Grablje had a magical atmosphere but the silence was unnerving. We walked seemingly back in time, strolling along ancient footpaths, climbing stone steps between crumbling houses and past an assortment of relics from past times, peeping into people's houses where they'd once lived their lives, homes that are gradually returning to nature. The roofs were caving in, the cobbled pathways overgrown with pretty wildflowers and herbs, every crumbling crevice occupied by lavender, rosemary, thyme, sage and oregano, providing a delicious array of Mediterranean scents. Bees, butterflies and lizards were the only living inhabitants.

Returning home, we found Bob sitting on our doorstep. Geoffrey knelt down beside him and gave him a biscuit. Thankfully he didn't have fleas. Bob, that is, not Geoffrey.

'I hope we don't see any more black cats,' commented Geoffrey, sipping on his non-craft beer.

After a successful morning of sightseeing around the island, we came back ready for a swim. The sun was beating down, the crops below wilting, not a breath of wind, perfect conditions in which to finally launch the great pineapple floatee. I'd bought the plastic beach pineapple on Korčula Island, only a massive storm meant the floatee had remained boxed. Incidentally, that's exactly where Geoffrey would have preferred it to stay.

Unpacking the box, Geoffrey was decidedly unimpressed with the pineapple's dimensions—2 metres long and 1.5 metres wide. He mentally calculated how much breath it was going to take to expand this gaudy piece of plastic monstrosity. He got a bit grumpy but I encouraged him from the sidelines by telling him to put some effort in. Finally we were set to go. Geoffrey went ahead, checking the coast was clear, closely followed by a scuttling, inconspicuous yellow and green pineapple with stubby legs protruding from the centre.

As I lurched down the typically sloping shingle beach, each of my feet sank further into the loose pebbles. My toes felt like they were being held by a giant suction cup. I was at risk of capsizing at any moment. Geoffrey solved the problem by throwing himself forward into the ocean. I faltered and called for help.

'I can't see where I'm stepping,' I shouted in alarm.

'Just look down. The water's so clear you can see everything.'

Alas the big green pineapple stalk to the front of me obscured all vision ahead. Geoffrey laughed unhelpfully and swam off. Sod it. I gave up and with all the grace of a hippo, threw myself forward, face-planted the stalk with a splat then headed to sea. Surprisingly my pineapple and I made it back to the shore without incident.

A couple of days later, I couldn't believe that I'd found myself back on board the very same vessel—the good ship *Marco Polo*—our family had spent a claustrophobic night aboard in a minuscule cabin in 2014. It was an experience not really to be repeated, but once again we were bound overnight for Ancona, Italy. It was late, very late, but I doubted sleep would come any time soon, cramped as I was in the narrow, hard bunk. I pondered the foolishness of my travel planning as the boat creaked and groaned in the darkness, dear Geoffrey once again snoring deeply above me, wedged into his tight-fitting, little bunk. I was sorely tempted to wedge a sock in his mouth. He was probably having nightmares over the grand entrance we made onto the ship.

Rolling over I tried to get comfortable on the stiff bed, chuckling over the irony of what had happened as we drove on board. I'm the first to admit that I'm usually to blame for many stressful situations. But this time I'd been falsely accused.

Things had started off so smoothly. Arriving on the dock at Split, we'd looked around in alarm at all the different ships, queues, barriers and multiple wharves. Geoffrey uttered those perfect little words, 'Oh shit.' But an angel in overalls had appeared in all his fluorescent-orange glory and guided us through barrier arms. Walking ahead of us, he waved us right to the front of a queue, ready to drive into the rear end of the *Marco Polo*. He then waved farewell and returned to his post. Whoever he was, I applauded his commitment to shepherding idiots. Next we had to leave the car and take my precious paper documents to the port office to exchange for tickets, use the loo, grab essential wine then dash back to the car.

There were only four cars about to board our old rust-tub, the *Marco Polo*. Ten port workers milled around, waiting for some invisible signal to begin loading the otherwise empty ship. Two cars were finally waved on board. Geoffrey naturally started ours, preparing to follow. A big, burly bloke stepped in front of us with his hand out and shouted, 'STOP.' It was as if two cars had overwhelmed their system.

A worker behind him waved at us to proceed up the steep metal ramp. Geoffrey engaged Cedric in gear and revved on the steep incline. This incensed the burly sailor who again yelled at us to 'STOP'. We were left revving precariously on the metal ramp with one worker saying, 'Come on,' and one shouting, 'Stop.'

'What the f#@%!' growled Geoffrey under his breath.

'I don't like it. We're going to roll backwards,' I screeched.

Finally one of the others tapped the burly sailor on the shoulder and he grudgingly stepped aside. With great relief, Geoffrey gave Cedric a rev and drove up the ramp and into the *Marco Polo*'s innards. Here we were led all the way to the pointy bow of the ship to an incredibly tight corner. The workers instructed Geoffrey in Italian on the art of positioning a Citroën hard up against as many obstacles as they could humanly find in an otherwise entirely empty hold.

Turning to me, Geoffrey snapped, 'Would you stop giving me orders? It's hard enough to concentrate without you sticking your oar in!'

'But I'm not talking,' I said indignantly. 'It's THEM,' I blurted angrily, pointing at the fastidious ferry workers trying to wedge us into a cookie box for absolutely no reason.

'Well whoever it is, I wish they'd shut up.'

I chuckled to myself in my bunk and hoped sleep would soon take me. Oh, and for anyone interested, when we returned to the car the next morning, there were still just the four vehicles sandwiched in the corner, skilfully parked in such a way that circus contortionism would be required to get back inside the cars.

'Never!' I gasped. 'You're not serious!' I stared wide-eyed at my friend over a coffee once Geoffrey and I were back at home.

She'd just informed me that my innocent pineapple had been somehow indicating to the world that Geoffrey and I were holidaying swingers. Leaving it to dry upside down apparently meant we were hosting a sex party. I slumped back in my seat, open-mouthed with horror, desperately trying to think if my pineapple had been drying upside down or not.

'And you didn't think to tell me this sooner?' I demanded.

2019

NEW CALEDONIA AND THAILAND

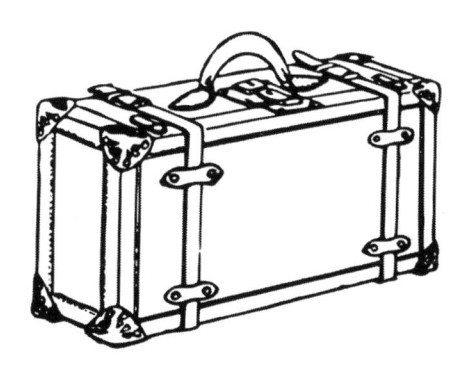

NANA'S SUITCASE

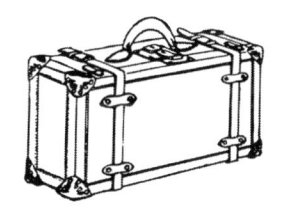

In 2019, eleven months after Poppa passed away, Jan and I took Nana on her first-ever trip on a cruise ship. In the years preceding Dad's death from asbestos lung cancer, my parents spent many happy hours at the wharf in Akaroa, happily watching guests come ashore off the big cruise ships. A favourite pastime of Nana's in particular was to see the ship tenders dock and motor back and forth. She was fascinated with the whole process but never imagined that one day she might get to experience this for herself.

Soon after Poppa passed away, Nana put her suitcase up in the rafters and announced that there were to be no more holidays for her; she was done.

'There's a Boxing Day sale on with Carnival Cruises,' Jan announced. 'Nine nights around New Caledonia, sailing out of Sydney. You could meet me when I finish my next cruise-ship contract.' Jan was home on shore leave before returning to her cruise-ship job, now based in Australia.

'Let's take Nana,' I said. I rang her and asked if she wanted to come on a cruise.

'I couldn't possibly,' she said, pausing. 'Could I?'

'Yes, you can. I'm booking it now,' I replied before she could back out.

We invited Geoffrey and Don but after the disastrous Southeast Asia cruise I'd dragged them on previously, they'd pretty much said they would rather stick pins in their eyes than ever set foot on a cruise ship again.

At the end of April, Nana's suitcase came down from the rafters once more. She and I flew across the Tasman Sea to Australia, landing in Sydney. The entire computer system that processes passengers died; airports were thrown into disarray. *Is it the curse of Denise? We're going to be stuck here for hours.* But not with my secret weapon—an old lady with a walking stick. We were pulled out of the queue and whizzed through customs and out to the arrivals hall. Nana was swamped by TV reporters eager for a scoop on the terrible effects of this massive system failure. Nana's response was a huge disappointment to the press and went like this:

'I had no problems at all. It was all fast and efficient.'

The reporters realised this wasn't the scoop they wanted and went to move away. But Nana wasn't finished with them. Jan had by now located us.

'And this is my granddaughter Jan. She works on cruise ships, you know. She has lots of cash.'

'Nana, stop,' wailed Jan and dragged us away. 'Nana, you made it sound like I was for sale,' she scolded once out of earshot.

The next morning a taxi delivered us to the overseas passenger terminal for our allotted boarding time. Stepping out of it, Nana and I peered up at the *Carnival Spirit*; she looked very grand. After we'd dropped our bags off and proceeded smoothly through the check-in process, we waited in a seated area for our call to board. I felt a moment of unease, thinking about the last and only cruise I'd ever been on: the posh, very expensive cruise from hell around Southeast Asia, complete with tiny cramped cabin, typhoon, abduction and illness. I prayed that this one would be different and secretly hoped that Nana was our good-luck charm. I believed Poppa would be right there with us, watching over us all and ensuring Nana had a good time.

Finally, the much-anticipated moment arrived. We walked up the ramp to the ship. Nana's walking stick was working overtime as she gazed all around with interest, eager finally to get a peek inside a cruise ship. Once on board we found our cabins and settled in. Well truthfully, Jan found them and we followed behind, looking bewildered. Oh, the relief to find large, spacious cabins. They even had room for a double couch and space to walk about. To our surprise we found we'd all been upgraded to rooms with extended balconies. I quietly thanked Poppa; our guardian angel had been busy.

Jan and I were sharing a cabin and Nana had her own just down the corridor. At 79 this was fabulously exciting for her; she was finally fulfilling a dream. As the ship set sail, Nana joined us on our balcony for our own sail-away party, complete with pre-ordered sparkling wine and crackers. Glasses clinked as we made a toast—cheers to a great holiday and cheers to cruising. It was 4 p.m. as we headed out towards the Sydney heads, gliding silently past the Sydney Harbour Bridge and the tiny ferries below. The lowering sun illuminated the sea like shimmering gold.

'Dolphins,' I shrieked with glee, watching enthralled as a pod of them rode the waves made by the bow of the ship directly below our balcony. As the dolphins escorted us out of the Sydney heads, I knew it was a sign Poppa was with us. This holiday was going to be magical and not the usual Denise shitshow.

The next day was a day at sea, spent exploring the ship. From the towering heights of the central atrium in gold and bronze tones, Nana and I marvelled at the glass lifts whizzing up and down. We toured the ship with our patient sea guide, Jan, who pretty soon realised that Nana and I couldn't find our way out of a paper bag. She became a guide for the permanently bewildered—her mother and Nana. Nana embraced it all with a sense of wonder: the food, the drinks, showtime in the dining room, amazing night-time entertainment, lounge bars, bingo and games. We did it all.

That night we assembled again on our balcony for what was to become our evening ritual of wine and crackers. Nana commented that it was a great sail-away party. Jan nearly choked on her cracker.

'But, Nana, how can it be a sail-away party? We're at sea. We aren't leaving port,' she laughed.

From then on, every night was nicknamed a sail-away party whether we were leaving a port or not.

Our first port of call was Nouméa, an overseas territory of France where the main language is French. This was one of Jan's regular working ports so she dragged her charges along with her to catch a local bus to the market. We shopped for outrageously bright and beautiful island print tops, drank coconut water directly from coconuts, listened to island music and examined exotic tropical fruits. Sitting in the shade of a palm tree, a happy trio, three generations, warm in the sun, we felt alive. Nana was thrilled with her day in Nouméa but what she was waiting for was the chance to go on a tender ride to shore.

The following morning we were greeted by the most stunning golden sunrise over a mirror-like sea. Peeping outside I noticed we were already anchored next to a pine-covered island, Mare Island in the Loyalty Island archipelago. As I stepped onto the balcony, I waved to Nana who was already outside, staring below. I looked down at the source of the clanking sound to see the tenders attached to the side of the ship being hydraulically extended and lowered to the sea below. Already busy, the workers were taking the tenders for a zip around on the water, testing all the engines. Nana watched them intently before disappearing into her cabin; she was off to get ready for breakfast.

We collected Nana on our way down the corridor. She was waiting, walking stick at the ready, but with an extra skip in her step; today she was going on a tender. She was going to be one of the cruise-ship passengers that others get to watch coming ashore. After breakfast we headed towards the lifts, expecting to have to queue for the ride. The cruise director, Linda, saw us coming, noticed Mum's walking stick and motioned us away from the queue.

'Good morning, lovely ladies. Come with me,' she said.

She took us to their private staff lift and escorted us down to the lower level then made everyone else wait while we three charmed ladies were sent ahead to the exit.

'Gosh, Nana, we'll have to bring you with us everywhere,' said Jan.

We couldn't believe our luck. As we walked onto the platform, many arms extended to assist Nana onto the waiting tender. We were all grinning but no one could look more chuffed than Nana, with a grin from ear to ear. She sat there like the Queen, commenting on everything going on around her from her perfect spot by the window. We bobbed along on the water, a jovial group of Australian and Kiwi families, for the short ride to shore. Our enthusiastic group disembarked to the sound of islanders singing and playing guitars in welcome, all dressed in their delightfully bright and cheerful clothing.

We boarded a bus to take us to Mare's main beach, Yedjele. The ride was exhilarating. There was no denying we were on a tropical island. We were travelling on a hard-packed dirt road with tropical vegetation all around. To our left were occasional glimpses of simple thatched-roof huts and houses in small village groups. To our right the vegetation intermittently parted, revealing a vista of sparkling, pure turquoise sea, surrounded by a fringe of distant white waves breaking on the reef. Beyond the protected reef, the water turned to a deeper indigo blue.

I glanced down at my beach bag nervously. Nana had achieved her dream this morning. Was I about to achieve mine? There, nestled in the beach bag alongside my towel and water shoes, sat two children's kickboards. I quivered inside, trying to give myself a pep talk. *Don't be embarrassed. Don't worry about what anyone thinks. This is your chance. You've trained for this. You know what to do. It will be OK. There are no sharks in there; it's a reef.*

At 52, a complete non-swimmer, I was about to attempt to snorkel over the reef. Oh heck, I was petrified. But Jan, a qualified swimming teacher, had given me lessons in our little, waist-deep, kit-construction Para Pool at home. I'd managed to stick my head under the water wearing the snorkel and to breathe calmly, at first just standing up with my face down, before progressing to floating using the kickboards stretched out in front of me for buoyancy. But this was different; this was the actual sea, with creatures in it, possibly sea snakes, deeper water and people-watching. *Oh shit, what if I panic and drown? What if the waves wash into the snorkel pipe?*

While this inner torment went on in my mind, the bus pulled up at paradise. Imagine a white-sand, palm-fringed, turquoise-ocean beach. All negative thoughts were chased away. We trotted off past the crowds, continuing to the far end of the beach where it was quieter. Nana, being the magic charm that she was, was offered a picnic table to sit at, shaded by a palm tree, where a local Mare islander was getting ready to crack open coconuts for the visitors. A delightful group of local ladies was setting up a stall of cold drinks and putting some chicken and rice on to cook. Perfect.

Nana, who never ventured into the water, was tempted in for a paddle before retreating to the shade of a palm while sipping from a coconut and watching us. I wondered to myself if she was on shark watch.

It was now or never but I didn't have time to think about it. Jan was calling me. Shoving my water shoes on, I removed my beach top and put on the snorkel and mask. Jan adjusted them for me. Taking the kickboards, we entered the water together. It was so warm and clear you could see the bottom. We walked out until it was waist-deep, where the coral began. Jan assured me she would stay with me and hold my rash top so I didn't float away. She was my anchor.

Shit, this is it, now or never. I did it. I pushed the boards in front of me, lifted my feet off the bottom and with a final prayer, I put my head down. All nerves were gone and I forgot about where I was. I forgot about my patient anchor, although every now and then I felt her dragging my leg or yanking my top when I started to drift away. I was gone. I was in a new and gob-smackingly beautiful world. For goodness' sake, there actually were fish down there. Who'd have thought it? I could see Nemo and Dory and the whole cast. There was purple coral, red, white, yellow and blue coral. I couldn't believe my eyes. There were fish going about their day in their private little world, darting in and out of the coral in a world that, until this moment, had been unseen by me except in photographs. I could've kicked myself. I'd waited 52 years to do this. What an idiot.

I popped up again and spat out the mouthpiece. Jan was tapping me. She wanted to go off and do some snorkelling of her own. I passed her my snorkel, babbling like an excited fool then went up to see Nana. The conversation started like this:

'You'll never guess what I saw down there?'

When Jan returned, our intrepid and adventurous trio enjoyed a lunch of smoky, fire-cooked chicken and parcels of rice, washed down with coconut water. But I was distracted. I had to get back into the sea. I couldn't leave without snorkelling again so we returned to the water.

'This is the start of my snorkelling career,' I announced.

'About bloody time,' said Jan.

Two dreams achieved in one day. I would remember this day for the rest of my life. Sitting on the bus heading back to the ship, I experienced a sensation I couldn't remember having since childhood: tired, sandy, matted salty hair, a touch of sunburn and feeling truly alive. Then Jan spoilt it.

'I saw a sea snake in the water,' she announced calmly.

'WHAT! Why didn't you tell me?' I demanded.

'You would never have gone back in,' she replied. She was right.

After a shower and another sail-away party, we three ladies donned our finest and went out to formal night. We walked through the ship to the dining room, stopping to step outside on deck. Before us, stretching as far as the eye could see, was a midnight-blue glass sea, as smooth as gentle folds of slowly undulating silk. The sun was setting on the horizon, melting into the sea, just a burnt-orange-and-red glow dipping below the horizon. A crisp crescent of moon had risen alongside one bright silver star, a perfect end to a perfect day.

The following day we awoke to a new island. This time we were anchored off Lifou, the largest and most populated island in the Loyalty archipelago. With our magic charm—Nana—along, we were once again whisked onto another short but fun tender ride across the luminous, emerald-green waters. Walking ashore we headed straight to the beach for an encore of snorkelling.

After drying off on the beach, we wandered up into the village for a walk around the market stalls then through the village streets. Perfume from exotic hibiscus flowers floated on the breeze as we passed tropical gardens. We decided to get a cup of tea from the local French-speaking Melanesian ladies in their bright, colourful dresses. They were selling cups of tea, banana fritters and tropical fruits.

Sitting in the large, thatched-roofed meeting house with our steaming cups of tea, we relaxed. The breeze wafted through the open-sided building, providing a little relief from the heat. We sat companionably, enjoying the atmosphere, the people-watching and the view out to sea, with the ship at anchor in the distance. Nearby was a rhythmic chopping of coconuts, providing coconut water to thirsty tourists. Happy chatter filled the air; a guitar played; locals and tourists alike shared a grassy slope to relax. Listening to the music, they contentedly munched on pawpaws, pineapples, mangos and banana fritters. Village dogs strolled and beautiful Melanesian ladies wearing colourful, ankle-length dresses sashayed through the crowd. All was well.

Our last port of call was Isle of Pines, an island of tall pine trees and white sandy beaches. The travel gods continued to shine down on us with blue skies, sunshine and warmth for our tender ride ashore. Nana was becoming an old hand at seafaring ways and a firm favourite with the delightful crew. She'd charmed our cabin attendant, found out his life story and had the dining-room maître d' round her little finger, ensuring us a good table each night.

Stepping ashore we were greeted by local Kanak people, dancing and singing in their dialect, welcoming the passengers. We boarded a bus with a beautiful guide, Eleni, who was dressed in a bright sky-blue dress. She was a natural: warm, modest, a little shy and with a smile that would brighten anyone's day. The bus toured the entire island, stopping in villages and points of interest along the way, giving us a glimpse of island life.

At Kuto Bay we swam in azure seas lapping a stretch of pure, crystal-white sand. Across the sand spit via a short track, we snorkelled over coral in Kanumera Bay. Here Jan towed me out to the coral reef in water that was over my head, keeping a firm hold on me. I gripped my kickboards tightly, imagining everything that moved was a sea snake. I soon signalled to Jan I'd finished. Weary, damp and salty, we returned to the pier. We thirstily drank the cold water we were offered before being whisked across the water to the *Carnival Spirit*.

That night at the sail-away party on our balcony, Nana asked, 'Which is the front of the boat?'

Jan spat her wine out, spluttering and coughing, before responding in an incredulous tone.

'Nana, we're literally sailing right now. You can see which way we're going so obviously that's the front,' she said, pointing to the bow. 'We're hardly going to reverse all the way back to Sydney.' We laughed as the sun slowly set on another fabulous day. The land was fading into the distance and we were homeward bound; just a sea day before docking in Sydney harbour at dawn the following morning.

Sadly all good holidays come to an end but with time on our hands before an evening flight, we caught a bus to Bondi Beach, hoping to catch a glimpse of the famous TV lifeguards. We'd only set foot on the beach for about 30 seconds before a seagull splattered poo on Nana's head.

'Bloody bugger,' she called out at it.

Jan and I doubled over in hysterics. Ten minutes later, after wiping Nana's head with her handkerchief, we sat down for a coffee and cake next to the beach. Sure enough, a pigeon landed on Nana's plate, pecked at her cake and pooed.

'Flaming Nora,' shouted Nana, screaming and flapping about.

'I think it's time to take Nana home again,' said Jan.

The holiday ended with three ladies in hysterics and I think a lesson to Nana that her life wasn't over; there was still fun to be had and future holidays to take. The suitcase was no longer kept in the rafters.

HONEE, YOU WAN' GEL NAILS?

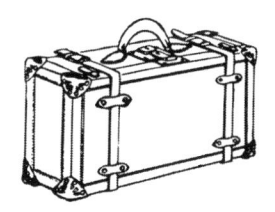

After our New Caledonia cruise, Jan returned to sea, sailing out of Brisbane and around the islands of Papua New Guinea until the end of the year. She then returned home to start working as a teacher at the same Early Childhood Centre as me.

Geoffrey and I meanwhile had itchy feet and empty wallets. A cheaper and closer-to-home destination was required. 'How about Thailand?' I suggested. Geoffrey wasn't sure but he didn't say no. I took that as a firm yes. Don was keen as long as it was after his university exams. Jan decided she wasn't going to miss out, despite having recently returned home, and promptly booked her flights.

I'd planned our visit with my usual thorough research. The monsoon season would be over in November. By December we would have warm, wonderful weather there, sunshine and calm seas. All through October I anxiously watched Thailand's weather. Where the heck was that monsoon? It remained unseasonably sunny. All through November my anxiety rose. The monsoon remained firmly absent.

On the 6th of December, 2019, Jan, Geoffrey and I arrived in Koh Samui; so did the monsoon. Don came with us in my suitcase. I was worried he would be discovered by customs' staff when they searched me in Sydney so I put a plastic bag over his head. I'll explain shortly.

Koh Samui, Thailand's second-largest island, lies in the Gulf of Thailand off the east coast of the Kra Isthmus, the narrowest part of the Malay Peninsula. It's known for its palm-fringed beaches, coconut groves and dense, mountainous rainforest. Luxury resorts and posh spas abound; we stayed at neither.

Instead we were at a $39-a-night, loosely termed 'resort' at the southern end of Lamai Beach which was great for the price. We had large, spacious, adjoining bungalows in a tropical garden setting. They were equipped with the fiercest air-con known to mankind, a shower open to view by the apartments behind, rock-hard beds and rickety, bamboo patio furniture covered in black mould. Perfect.

Upon arrival in the room, I let Don out of the suitcase. He'd survived the journey intact on his stick. I couldn't have a family holiday without Don. I raised his head and we took a family selfie with a photo of Don's head glued firmly to a piece of cardboard and attached to an ice-block stick. CHEESE! Don had been awarded a summer scholarship job, which was fantastic but meant he wasn't able to come with us.

Geoffrey tied a sarong over the bathroom window, preventing us from being filmed in the shower and inadvertently making an unwanted appearance on some dodgy Thai YouTube channel. So that eye-catching problem was easily overcome. And apart from the air-con, the other issues were minor. We found the Thai staff to be delightfully friendly and hospitable. They were patient and helpful with our attempts to learn as many basic Thai words as we could master.

A walk along a path through the lush green garden brought us to a minuscule, green-tiled pool surrounded in tatty, fake grass. We weren't bothered by this as we planned to spend all our time at the beach. The entire place appeared deserted. Next to the pool were the restaurant and steps to the beach just below. We stood and surveyed it with dismay. Waves thundered to the shore and creamy, sand-flecked sea foam flew through the air. Despite the lack of sun, I felt like I was draped in a hot, damp towel. Dark-black, threatening skies stretched across the horizon. This wasn't supposed to happen. *Not to worry. It will be different tomorrow.*

Back in our room later that night, I switched the air-conditioner on, startled by the sudden sound of a Boeing engine emanating around the place.

'Jeez,' muttered Geoffrey, gripping his book as a force-10 blizzard shot across the room, scattering loose papers.

The air-con appeared to have only one setting—gale force. The meagre one sheet and a thin bedcover weren't going to be enough to deal with this. Geoffrey lay in the teeth of the gale, layered in beach towels, knowing not to mess with menopause. The air con needed to stay on for everyone's sanity.

The next morning at breakfast, as we ate our platter of beautiful tropical fruits, we stared out forlornly at the sea. The sea foam was now being driven halfway up the steps from the beach in great billowy waves of white cotton candy. The clear plastic rain blinds had been rolled down around the restaurant facing the sea. They billowed in and out, smacking against the bamboo poles. Raindrops from a passing shower drummed against the plastic. The monsoon had come late this year. In fact, according to our cheerful Thai waiter, it had arrived the day we did. Another case of the universe having a laugh at Denise, I suspect.

After breakfast, Geoffrey decided that, being a strong swimmer, he would tackle the waves and have a refreshing swim. Jan and I watched dubiously from the shelter of a tree at the edge of the beach. Sea foam licked at our toes. Geoffrey walked a couple of feet into the angry surf. A big wave picked him up and dumped him on his bum, where he was rolled over and over in the water. He staggered from the sea, spitting sand out of his mouth. Over the roar of the howling wind and crashing waves, we heard Geoffrey shout, 'Retreat.' We scuttled back up the froth-covered steps to the hotel.

Undefeated, Geoffrey decided to test the deserted pool. His feet skidded on the slippery bottom, disturbing a layer of algae which gently floated to the surface around him. *Oh, so the pool doesn't have green tiles after all*, I realised. *It's just scum.*

'Oh for goodness' sake,' groaned Geoffrey, gingerly climbing back up the slippery ladder.

Jan and I burst out laughing. 'Dad, you've got green legs,' she said, giggling. Sure enough, a sample of algae had stuck to his leg hairs.

With water activities over for the day, Jan decided to have a massage at the resort's beach shack then get her nails done while Geoffrey and I took a walk around our end of Lamai Beach township. Further down the main road, we followed a lane bordered with lots of little souvenir stalls and tourist shops which led us down to a rocky point on the beach. We stopped and stared. Before us was a realistic, giant penis-shaped rock. And according to the sign, somewhere among the rocks was a vagina waving to the ocean.

Locally known as Hin Ta and Hin Yai, grandfather and grandmother rocks, their resemblance to genitalia has made them one of the strangest tourist attractions in the world. According to local legend, these rock formations are all that remain of an old couple that washed ashore in a storm.

'Right,' said Geoffrey with raised eyebrows.

'Shall we look for the vagina?' I asked.

But Geoffrey had already turned to head back. He was probably wondering why I'd dragged him 6,000 miles from home for this. A window display full of crabs caught my attention on the way. Minutes later I was the proud owner of a new family of crabs. Each delicate little hermit crab had been lovingly crafted out of coloured glass. A psychologist might deduce that the five-year-old Denise was still riled over losing her crabs on the bus. We walked back to our bungalow, with me proudly clutching my precious box of crabs. Jan was already there.

'I need a cup of tea,' said Geoffrey.

'You can't. The power's out,' Jan replied. Geoffrey sighed deeply.

'You were quick,' I said to Jan.

'Due to the wind, the power went out halfway through doing my nails. I've only got one hand done.' She laughed, showing us one hand of brightly painted nails. 'What have you two been doing?'

'I got crabs and we saw a giant dick on the beach,' I announced, chortling at my joke. Jan stared at me and rolled her eyes. 'D'you wanna see my crabs?' I asked, laughing cheekily.

That night we ate down the road at the Lucky Elephant where the waitress doubled as the nail lady. Between courses Jan went with the waitress to get her nails finished now that the power was back on. Geoffrey and I grinned, finding this amusing. Only in Thailand. While waiting, we studied the menu. The vegetarian mains caught my eye: chicken or pork soup, pad Thai with chicken or pork, Panang curry with chicken or pork, massaman curry with chicken or pork; in fact whatever you liked, as long as it had chicken or pork in it to make it vegetarian. Interesting concept.

Walking home after dinner, we dodged fast-moving tuk-tuks and scooters as we gingerly dashed across the busy road. The sound of chirping crickets reverberated around us in the moisture-laden air. Down the alleyway, we entered the unlit garden path to our bungalow. Movement in the shadows caught our attention. Torch light revealed toads staring back at us. Rustling in the trees overhead conjured up images of snakes. We walked faster.

The wind picked up once we were in bed; torrential rain fell in sheets. As we lay in bed with a cup of tea, we heard an almighty thud on the roof, followed by a clunky rolling sound as something heavy tumbled down and crash-landed on our deck outside.

'Shit,' said Geoffrey, gazing up.

'D'you think a monkey fell out of the tree?' I asked, getting out of bed to investigate.

I grabbed my torch and shone it outside the window. A massive coconut was on our doorstep. The power went out again. We drank our tea in the darkness without comment.

The next day the water was off but the power was on. That was swimming and showering off the resort menu. Geoffrey was really pleased I'd brought him to Thailand. The storm raged on so we went for a drive around the island. Heading inland, away from the tourist areas, we were quickly enveloped in large swathes of tropical rainforest and coconut plantations interspersed with small villages and towns. Each village had a decorative Buddhist temple as a place of worship.

The road eventually led us to the sleepy fishing village of Thong Krut, set in a sweeping bay. Traditional, wooden longtail boats floated in teal-coloured water, each boat adorned with colourful ribbons tied onto the bow. These decorations look pretty but are there to provide good luck and protection. In Thailand there's a strong belief in spirits, and the bright garlands at the front of the boat are in honour of the water spirits and Mae Ya Nang, the goddess of journeys.

When I stepped out of the car for a walk along the beach, my hair blew sideways. Sand slapped against my ankles in a blast of warm air as though a hairdryer was directed at my skin. A French boulangerie built on wooden stilts out over the water offered us an ideal refuge from the wind. As we sat on the deck, sipping from coconuts, the wooden deck railings formed a perfect frame for the colourful longtail boats, flawlessly capturing this typical Thai scene.

Later, upon returning home to our bungalows, Jan headed off for another massage. Geoffrey lounged on the bed reading and I went out to sit on the deck. Closing my eyes I listened to the soft call of the birds. Rustling sounds from above caught my attention. As I peered up into the treetops, I was surprised to see a couple of little squirrels scampering across the branches. I had no idea they had squirrels in Thailand. I called out to Geoffrey to come and look but grumpy was too busy enjoying time without me and the air-conditioner. I closed my eyes again.

Something tickled my toes. I shot out of the chair like a bullet, imagining a tarantula. From the safety of the doorway, I looked back. An army of ants steadily marched across our deck. That was enough nature for me. I retreated indoors and whacked the air-con on. Geoffrey sighed and drew the towels around him. Jan arrived back from her massage.

'You should come next door, Dad,' she said. 'It's nice and warm.'

Geoffrey needed no encouragement. He grabbed his book and headed to Jan's room.

'Rude,' I called after them.

I rechecked the air-con remote. It wasn't as if I'd set it to my usual optimum menopause temperature of 16 degrees. It was currently on 25 but it felt like the Arctic, even to me. I got bored and wandered next door. The buggers had locked me out. Laughing, Jan reluctantly opened the door. Geoffrey didn't look up from his book.

'Jeepers, it's like a furnace in here,' I wailed and left again.

We discovered that the island's western side was sheltered from the wind and waves rolling in from the Gulf of Thailand. Here at the crescent-shaped Lipa Noi Beach, we swam in calmer waters. Palm fronds formed moving shadows across the crunchy, golden crystals of sand. Fallen coconuts littered the beach alongside assorted storm debris. The sky was still a threatening shade of purple, and soft warm rain continued to fall. The ocean felt like a silky turquoise bath. We swam alone at the beach, afterwards dashing, dripping wet, to the car as another squall rolled in. *This wasn't how it was meant to be*, I told myself once again.

Inclement weather didn't stop us from finding things to do. With Buddhism being the main religion on the island, magnificent temples were plentiful. Night markets were full of exotic tastes and smells, colours and music. I learnt that an undercooked silk worm is not a crunchy taste sensation as I was led to believe by Jan. The worm's guts and poop burst all over my salivary glands; it was spectacularly awful.

At Coco Tam's bar, I discovered it's not a good idea to smother your hair in excessive hairspray before attending a beach fire show. I came close to becoming an encore act—Denise the Human Torch. How was I supposed to know the fire dancers walk into the crowd swinging their kerosene-soaked flaming ropes over everyone's heads? It was just lucky the dancers spotted Geoffrey raising our water jug, ready to throw over my scalp, and backed off. They thought the grumpy twit was about to toss a jug of water at them.

Finally after days of monsoonal rain, the weather cleared a couple of days before we left and we took our first walk along Lamai Beach. Not far from our accommodation, we came to The Black Pearl Bar and Restaurant where we enjoyed their sunbeds, food and drinks on the sparkling beach.

While we were lying there, an old Thai woman carrying her nail caddy approached Geoffrey and grabbed his gnarly feet, staring at his hobbit-like toes.

'You sexy mann, woteva you like, I do for youuu?' she crooned. Geoffrey stared at her in horror. 'Honee, you want pedicure?'

'No!' exclaimed Geoffrey, looking aghast and trying to wrench his horrid toes from her grasp. Jan and I looked on with grinning faces.

'Honee, don' worree. I fix for you, make you sexeey,' she breathed, leaning in. We chortled at Geoffrey's discomfort. 'Honee, what you need today? I give massage. You have boyfrien'?'

'No, I do not,' cried Geoffrey and we howled with laughter. She was clearly playing with him, enjoying this as much as we were. She winked over at Jan and me.

'Don' worry, honee. You like cry'tal gel nails?' she asked, grabbing his hand.

'What?' gasped Geoffrey. 'Whatever that is, no, I do not.'

'Honee, relaxxx, don' worree. I fix for you,' she crooned. She moved to his stomach. 'You big boy,' she said, patting her stomach and pushing it out to emphasise its shape. Jan and I now had tears of laughter rolling down our cheeks.

Poor Geoffrey, red-faced, was saved by the arrival of our lunch and the waiter telling the woman to sling her hook. That didn't stop Jan and me from teasing him mercilessly over lunch.

'My stomach's not that big,' muttered Geoffrey.

Over lunch, Jan reminded me of when we were sitting on the beach in Cambodia the year before and I'd foolishly invited a nail lady over. We all laughed at the memory.

'Dad and I just stayed in the water until the vendors had gone,' said Jan. 'It was your own stupid fault. We keep telling you not to keep talking to people.'

This was true. I love to meet people but soon regretted it on this occasion. I didn't realise all the other beach vendors would sense a sucker and swoop en masse. I quickly found myself surrounded, a lady on either side, each giving me the worst nail job ever.

Next to arrive was the leg lady, approaching Don and me, viciously waving around a piece of wire and threatening to scrape the hairs off our legs. Don shot me a filthy look and acted fast. Quick as a flash, he whipped a towel around his legs, clamping the sides down firmly. Not sure how to deal with this mortifying situation his mother had caused, he pulled out his book and stared resolutely at it, refusing all further attempts at communication. I think he was reading *50 Ways to Kill Your Mammy*. And right then, I couldn't blame him.

With my hands out of action, I was helpless. The lady moved fast, swiftly grabbing my defenceless legs. Kneeling in front of me, she examined them closely, looking horrified at my untidy, prickly leg hairs. Before the filthy wire thread could maim me, I decided cash was the only course of action here. Share the money out and get nail lady to call off her mob. I knew I'd made a grave error in calling her over. How was I to know all her friends would appear from behind the palm trees? I paid the mob off and they departed happy. Geoffrey and Jan emerged from the sea, laughing. Don was furious with me. I looked down at my gaudily painted nails. Splodges of clumpy red polish dotted my fingernails, each hand a different colour. There was more polish on my fingers than my nails.

'And they've done a shit job too!' I muttered. 'What a flipping mess.'

2020

NEW ZEALAND

FECKER THE FALCON'S WILD RIDE

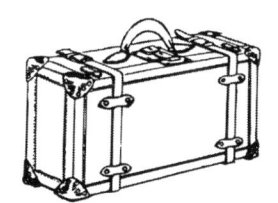

*I*t was the first week of January 2020 and Nana was about to turn 80. Because Poppa had passed away 18 months earlier, her big occasion was tinged with sadness. As far as she knew, we were going out for a Chinese to celebrate her birthday. As if! We all wanted to make it special so I hatched a plan. Unbeknown to Nana, Helen and family would be flying up to surprise her at a mystery location.

A couple of days before her birthday, I presented Nana with a piece of paper. It said she needed to pack a suitcase as we were taking her away for the weekend. The destination was a surprise, but a packing list was enclosed with tips on what she would need to bring. Helen and family played their parts beautifully, pretending they didn't know where we were taking her, not a clue. They continued to put Nana off the scent by mentioning their own plans on that same weekend. She had no inkling that they would be boarding a flight to Wellington right when we were picking her up to leave on the surprise trip.

We pulled up at Nana's house in Geoffrey's beat-up, old Ford Falcon, commonly referred to as Fecker the Falcon. It was summer and my own car's air-con wasn't working so we'd decided to take Geoffrey's old dunger. Actually, let me rephrase that. It was me; it was a Denise decision. Anyway, Geoffrey's car was disgusting but it had air-con. I'm not sure why I thought we needed it. Our destination was the Chateau Tongariro, 1,100 metres up the side of an active volcano, Mount Ruapehu.

Nana came out to the car, walking stick in hand, grinning from ear to ear with excitement.

'Your white chariot fit for a queen awaits you,' I announced. Well, it was white; that was the only truth in the statement.

Geoffrey brought her big suitcase out and opened the boot. Nana gasped at the sight of all the luggage. Where was her case supposed to fit? Thankfully Fecker was an ex-taxi, an ancient workhorse with a roomy boot, used to carting heavy loads. With a bit of rearranging, Geoffrey, master packer extraordinaire, proudly slammed the boot shut. One of the kids had noticed the large container of water among the luggage and asked what it was for.

'The engine,' said Geoffrey.

I had no time to question him as we were caught up in the rush and excitement of the moment. The universe chuckled; it would save this for later.

Nana climbed in and the kids helped her with her seat belt. She paused to get her breath back and stared aghast at the ceiling, or lack of it. The fabric had long since parted company with the roof structure. All that remained was a sagging remnant and blobs of brown fabric glue. Her eyes took in the smashed wing mirrors, looking much like a glass mosaic. To complete the look, there were spiders' webs and dead bugs decorating the interior.

'Good Lord,' she exclaimed, looking around. 'Are you sure this thing is going to make it to wherever we're going?'

'Yes, don't worry,' I said, climbing in. 'At least it has air-con.' I adjusted the cushion I was sitting on. Geoffrey and I had to perch on them as the front seats' upholstery was dissolving into the floorboards. Nana took out her handkerchief and used it to wipe cobwebs off her window with a look of distaste.

And off we went, into the unknown, our family of four and Nana. As we reached the highway and turned north, Nana texted her best friend, Judy, to update her on the direction then announced, 'I know where we're going. We're going to Lake Taupō.' We remained silent, not giving away the surprise. Destination sorted in her mind, she sat back to enjoy the journey.

At Waiouru, her confidence faltered when we turned off and headed left towards Ohakune instead of directly towards Taupō. Her phone came out again as she texted Judy with the change of direction. Judy replied, 'You must be going to the Chateau.' Nana read out the text and we laughed at this preposterous idea.

'As if we could afford that posh place,' we said.

And looking around the car, Nana could quite believe it. No, we were just avoiding roadworks, we told her. She was satisfied with this explanation. I dozed off.

'Jeepers,' shouted Nana from the back seat, closely followed by Jan screaming and a resounding 'thwack'. A spider had strolled across Nana's window sill and promptly been splattered by her handbag.

'Ooh, gross,' said Jan.

Don ignored them and kept his headphones on, largely so that Nana couldn't keep interrogating him about girls.

Geoffrey, unbeknown to us, was becoming alarmed by the old clunker's performance. No, not Nana! The temperature gauge was going up and down randomly (well, actually, that describes me). Each time we went uphill, it overheated (again, me) and he was pleased he'd brought the container of water to top up the radiator if needed. Fecker valiantly limped on and Geoffrey didn't say anything to spoil the happy mood in the car.

Texting Helen, Nana updated her on our direction and said she was pretty certain we were heading to Taupō. I gazed out at the spectacular scenery; we were now driving through the Tongariro National Park, a unique volcanic alpine plateau. Meanwhile Helen and her family had arrived in Wellington and were setting off in a four-wheel-drive rental car, following a couple of hours behind us. As we drove through National Park village, I announced that I needed to go to the toilet, all part of my plan to put Nana off the scent. As we approached the turnoff to Chateau Tongariro, I asked Geoffrey to take me on a quick detour to use the Chateau's facilities.

Nana was horrified. 'You can't go to the Chateau just to use their toilets,' she gasped.

'Yes I can. They're open to day visitors so I'm sure they won't mind.'

'Can't you just hold on till Taupō?' argued Nana.

Too late, there she was—the grand, five-storey hotel built in 1894, nestled against the lower slopes of Mount Ruapehu volcano and containing 134 sumptuous rooms, a grandiose lounge, dining and reception rooms. Geoffrey pulled up under the elegant portico rather than in the car park, knowing we were actually checking in and would need to offload a mountain of luggage.

This was too much for Nana. She leant forward in alarm. 'You *can't* stop here in the entrance just to use their toilet; this is for guests.' She groaned. But I was off out through the door, calling out that I would be back in a minute.

Check-in complete, I returned to the car where Nana was still fretting at my audacity. I nodded at Geoffrey who hopped out to start unloading the bags from the boot.

'Right, you can get out of the car; we've arrived at our destination,' I announced, opening the car door for Nana.

'Really?' she gasped. 'Are we staying here, at the Chateau? Really, or are you just tricking me?'

'Nope, it's real, come on. We've got our keys so we can go find our rooms, oh, and SURPRISE!' I added.

Geoffrey quickly took the old heap to the car park then trotted back to us. We put our bags on a trolley and walked inside, with Nana still dithering about in disbelief. At the same time, she was trying to text Judy to tell her she really *was* staying at the Chateau.

We went up in the lift to the second floor where Helen and I had organised for Nana to have a beautiful room with a lovely view of the mountains. Leaving Nana exclaiming over everything and unpacking, we went to find our own broom-closet rooms around the corner. The kids were paying for their accommodation and couldn't afford the twin room so they had to have a basic double. They immediately assembled a barricade down the middle of the bed, with Jan issuing dire warnings to Don that if so much as one little toe crossed onto her side, he was dead meat.

In the company of HRH Nana, we descended via the fancy, red-carpeted staircase to the elegant lounge. After making our grand entrance, we seated ourselves comfortably on the plush, red couches. Swathes of red and gold fabric decorated the room, matched with rich, wood-grain furniture and antiques. We looked around in awe at the enormous fireplace in front of us and the huge paintings. A waiter wearing an elegant suit brought us an extensive gin and tonic menu to peruse. We selected delicious-sounding gin and mixes which arrived on a silver tray.

Meanwhile my excitement was building. Helen texted to say they were getting close, just turning off at National Park and would be pulling up shortly. I was sitting facing towards the mountains and could see the car park from my seat. Not long after, I saw my nephew and niece climb out of a vehicle and head towards the hotel entrance. Telling Nana I was just going to reception to grab a couple of walking maps, I hurried out to meet them. With whispered hugs, beaming faces and silly grins, we couldn't wait to see Nana's face when she saw them.

Triumphant, I proudly led them back into the lounge towards Nana. She was sitting facing us and looked up. My nephew, Sean, was at the front, followed by my niece, Shayla. Nana's mouth dropped open, her face registering complete shock. Eyes wide, she pointed towards Sean in disbelief, yelling out, 'It's Sean, what? Sean, what are you doing here?' she snapped at him, leaping up, her face beaming, delight showing in her eyes. 'Shayla.' She laughed aloud as Shayla stepped into view, rushing to grab both of them in a warm embrace.

Helen appeared behind them. 'I don't believe it. Helen's here too,' Nana called out, 'and Murray. Where did you all appear from?' With hugs complete, Nana flopped back onto the couch and reached for her gin.

'Well, cheers to that,' she declared.

'Thank goodness we can finally stop all the lies,' I exclaimed.

We called the waiter over for another round of drinks and everyone talked at once. Helen and Murray went to check in and take their bags up to their rooms while we filled Nana in on all the details of our dastardly plan. Poring over walking maps, we planned our weekend, everyone chatting, sipping gin, laughing and happy. Nana texted Judy to update her on the latest developments. Eventually we dispersed to our rooms before meeting in the lounge later to go out for dinner.

After breakfast the next morning, we dressed warmly and headed up the mountain. The drive up through the volcanic landscape of Mount Ruapehu was spectacular, featuring colourful silica terraces, old lava flows and dramatic waterfalls. Nana drove up with Helen and family in the four-wheel drive. Meanwhile inside our old jalopy, Geoffrey's brow was furrowed in consternation as he watched the temperature gauge creeping upwards. When I climbed out of Fecker at the top of the road, my nose detected the unmistakable smell of burning.

However, all thoughts of car troubles were quickly forgotten as we looked around in wonder. Whakapapa skifield base resembled what I can only imagine landing on Mars would look like. We were about to journey into the clouds on the Sky Waka with 360-degree views around the majestic Mount Ruapehu. At the top was Knoll Ridge Chalet, New Zealand's highest dining experience at 2,020 metres. We all climbed aboard two gondolas and were lifted over vast black and rust-red volcanic debris, and waterfalls gushing down the mountain. Mists swirled around us. My family could see Nana and Helen's brood behind us in the following gondola, staring around them in awe.

Our excited group stepped off the gondolas and out into a mountain landscape of snow and volcanic boulders surrounded by craggy peaks. The kids took off in all directions, ecstatic to explore in the snow. They were closely followed by Helen, camera clicking, trying in vain to get them all to pose for photos. They threw snowballs at her in return, amid much laughter. Nana and I sat atop a boulder where we could watch it all, Nana grinning widely. Eventually our exhilarated party regrouped and headed into Knoll Ridge Chalet to Pātaka Café where we enjoyed hot drinks and cake in front of floor-to-ceiling windows with vast, mountaintop panoramic views.

Snowflakes began to fall lightly, dancing around us as we stepped out onto the terrace, hands outstretched catching snowflakes, faces smiling, Helen's camera clicking to preserve this moment. We were spellbound. It was January, mid-summer; this wasn't supposed to happen. I felt Poppa was with us, wanting Nana's birthday celebrations to be special. I smiled; this was perfect.

When we got back to the hotel, Geoffrey popped out to the car to top up the radiator with water. He was surprised to find it didn't need any. He checked the coolant. There was no leak so why was Fecker overheating? There wasn't time to ponder this further.

After lunch we walked to Tawhai Falls, an iconic waterfall used as a film location in *The Lord of the Rings*. Later we assembled in the Chateau's grand drawing room, wearing our finery for Nana's 80th-birthday high tea. She was treated like a queen, presented with gifts while we ate delicate, fancy small bites and sipped tea and champagne.

As I lay in bed the next morning, I was gazing out upon Ngauruhoe volcano set against a startlingly blue sky when Geoffrey interrupted my reverie.

'Fecker's stuffed,' he announced. 'He won't make it back.'

Snapping out of my tranquil mood, I stared at Geoffrey. He explained his worries about the old banger's ability to make the journey home. His opinion was that if we risked it and headed off, Fecker would likely break down in the middle of nowhere, leaving us stranded. We could either take the gamble or call the AA. No, Fecker didn't have a drinking problem, although he was rather fond of water. I mean the Automobile Association.

Decision made, Geoffrey called the AA to place a breakdown call and we waited for someone to ring us back. I leapt out of bed and got dressed, wondering how to break the news to Nana that her queen's chariot was really just a big, rusty heap of junk after all. Geoffrey's phone rang. Perching on the side of the bed, I listened intently. It was decided, based on Fecker's symptoms, that a roadside repair wasn't an option. Fecker needed to go to a garage. They would find the nearest available twin-cab tow truck and call us when it was on its way. Geoffrey hung up.

Downstairs at breakfast we informed the family that Geoffrey's knackered heap of a car was broken and we were being collected from the stately Chateau Tongariro by a tow truck. Oh, the humiliation. There were gasps of horror although the kids, mercifully used to our travel woes, took it in their stride and thought it was hysterically funny. Nana did not. We arranged for her to travel home in style in Helen's four-wheel drive. They would drop her at home on their way to the airport. Breakfast was a sombre affair.

We said our goodbyes to the family. The tow-truck driver was on his way and would arrive in about 30 minutes. We hopped in the sorry excuse of a car and drove it from the car park to the front of the Chateau where the tow truck would have room to manoeuvre. We sat inside Fecker's dank interior; the brown-stained ceiling practically touched our heads as the resident spiders looked at us inquisitively. There we sat and waited miserably, feeling like down-and-outers who couldn't afford an actual chariot. Where was our fairy godmother with a giant pumpkin in hand? *This wasn't meant to happen*, I thought glumly.

Then came what I thought was the final humiliation. A great big tow truck pulled up in front of the Chateau's dining-room windows, in full view of all the guests dining and sipping coffee. We hopped out of Fecker and unloaded our luggage to the pavement. There we stood, a sorry little group of losers getting picked up from the stately Chateau by a tow truck. We were clearly not Chateau-type guests. The driver told us to climb aboard.

Oh shit, not again. The cab was nearly at the height of my waist. There was no way my little legs could climb up there. Images of the Mount Cook Land Rover incident flashed through my mind. Somehow I needed to get into this thing. Spying the luggage, I got Geoffrey and the kids to lay a big suitcase flat on the ground next to the cab. All eyes at the Chateau's dining-room windows were now upon this short, tubby lady who appeared to be using a suitcase as a springboard.

I stepped on it. Nope, still not high enough. Another suitcase was added to my tower and then another to make a series of steps. Heads craned as my audience, with bated breath, watched this most absurd spectacle as I clambered precariously up my tower of luggage. Don and Jan had hopped in the other side of the truck by now. So Don pulled and Geoffrey pushed. Finally the eagle landed. I made it in, just in time to look up and wave goodbye to Nana and the family. They cruised past ever so slowly, taking it all in and laughing hysterically. *Do not look towards the Chateau windows*, I willed myself. *Do not look.*

'Jeez, everyone's staring,' groaned the kids with embarrassment.

Crash, bang, thump. Fecker the Falcon was getting clamped behind the truck. Geoffrey tossed the suitcases into the back with us and clambered into the front cab alongside the driver. We were ready to depart. I looked at Jan and Don and we all burst out laughing. What else was there to say?

Geoffrey asked the driver where he was taking us. Only as far as a garage in Ohakune. After that, if the car couldn't be repaired, we would have to make travel arrangements to get home. Oh shit. Ohakune was over 230 kilometres from where we lived. How the hell were we meant to get back? We all grabbed our cell phones and started googling our options. There was one train a day. We were too late for that. There was a bus we might make in time. No, it was fully booked. Was there a car rental? Nope. We needed Fecker to be repaired or we were as stuffed as he was.

Once we reached Ohakune, the driver pulled in at the garage. Fecker the Falcon, passengers and luggage were dumped at the side of the road and the tow-truck driver departed. Geoffrey went to talk to the mechanic while the kids and I dragged our suitcases over to a nearby bench to wait for news. We sat lost in thought. Well, one thought really: if Fecker couldn't be fixed, how the hell were we going to get home? So far we hadn't come up with a single solution.

The mechanic called Geoffrey over; he'd found the problem. The thermostat had seized in the shut position, not allowing coolant to circulate. He was able to open it. Fecker was good to go; luggage and passengers were reloaded and we were off.

Nana texted to say her fine new chariot had delivered her safely to her house where Helen and her family were now enjoying a nice cup of tea, fit for a queen.

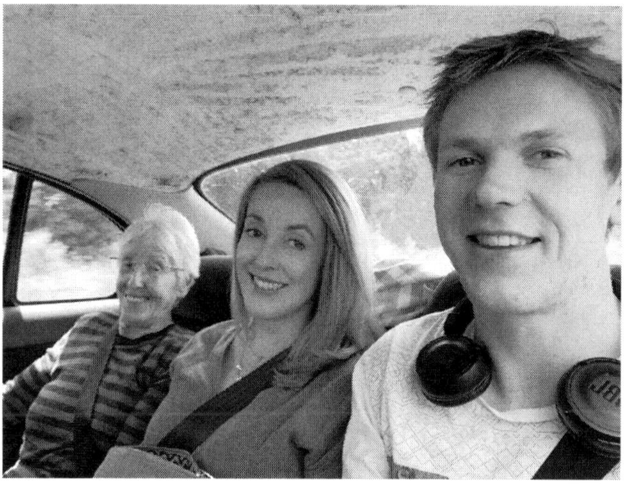

COVID TOES AND COVID WOES

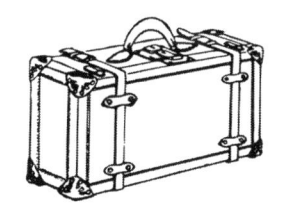

This chapter provides a fitting finale to this travel memoir, given that the worldwide COVID pandemic temporarily halted our travels. New Zealand slammed its borders shut and we all hunkered down within our own wee bubble for the next two years. Here are some of my family's lighter moments from the start of the pandemic, followed by a COVID holiday disaster.

'Duty nurse speaking. How can I help you?'

'Ah yes, good morning. I think my son has COVID toes,' I said, going red with embarrassment. Both Jan and Don sat giggling in the background, finding this most entertaining. There was a stunned silence on the other end of the phone. I cringed. Blimmin' Don and his stupid toes.

'Madam, I don't understand. Did you just say COVID toes?' she asked.

'Ah yes, that's right. I'd better explain.'

'Yes, please, but I need to pop you on hold for a minute,' she said, sounding incredulous.

I covered the mouthpiece.

'This is *your* fault, Jan. I wouldn't even be in this embarrassing position if it wasn't for you sending me that stupid photo and the story on COVID toes from the news. They're not my toes. I don't see why I'm the one who has to ring the doctor's surgery and be humiliated,' I said.

'Well, I'm not ringing them,' grumbled Don.

'Me neither,' said Jan.

'They clearly think I'm a lunatic. I bet she's put me on hold so she can have a laugh. She's probably shouted it out to everyone there.'

'OK, madam, go ahead. You were saying you think your son has COVID toes?' the nurse enquired.

'Yes, well, my son's just come home from Wellington for the lockdown and he's got a funny red rash on his toes. Then my daughter read online about COVID toes and sent me a picture. They look just like Don's toes,' I explained. Saying it out loud just made it sound even more ridiculous.

'What exactly are COVID toes?' she asked.

'I'll read it out to you. I've got the article here. "COVID toes are a potential symptom linked to COVID-19 that is mostly showing up in young people. It presents as a reddish-purple rash on the toes",' I read. 'There are photos with the article and they look just like Don's feet,' I added.

There was a long pause on the other end of the phone before the nurse asked if I could email through some photos of Don's toes.

'I just don't believe I'm doing this.' I groaned as I leant in close, hovering over Don's size-12 hooves with my phone. I clicked away, moving him onto the deck where the sunlight could highlight his gnarly digits and pick up the purple-red rash. Jan laughed away in the background. As far as lockdown entertainment went, this was the most interesting thing to happen in a while.

'You didn't have to call the doctor,' commented Jan.

'Well, what sort of mother would I be if I ignored it and his toes ended up dropping off?'

Geoffrey stepped out of his office for a lunch break and gave me a questioning glance on seeing me on the deck photographing Don's feet. He seemingly decided he didn't want to know and scuttled off quick as lightning.

With the toes finally artfully presented in photographic form, I emailed the pictures off to the doctor's surgery, imagining the response at the other end. I really didn't know how I would ever show my face there again.

The doctor rang back about an hour later and said she thought Don just had a fungal infection. She would email through a prescription for a cream which we could collect from the pharmacy.

'Jeez, Mum, you're so embarrassing,' said Jan.

'Don't you give me that. This was all your doing!' I retorted.

Geoffrey reappeared hesitantly from his office.

'What's going on?' he asked.

'Mum rang the doctor's and told them Don has COVID toes,' chortled Jan.

'It's not funny,' snapped Don. 'They're really itchy.'

'And guess what, Dad? She even sent them photos of his toes.' She laughed hysterically.

During this time of uncertainty and fear during the pandemic, I became paranoid about protecting my family. I can still hear Geoffrey's dulcet tones yelling out to no one in particular.

'What's happened to the TV?'

'Why's the light blown in the pantry?'

'Why won't the lamp work?'

'Who's been fiddling with my keyboard?'

Shamefaced, I owned up to my dawn activities—Denise strikes again. With damp cloth and bleach in hand, I was setting off on a daily COVID-destroying mission: light switches, remotes, handles and keyboards, all drowned in a liberal bleach bath. I was saving my family's lives, damnit, so what if the TV was now dead, along with a keyboard and an assortment of lights? We were clean. But if anyone dared leave the house, I would have to do my rounds again. I admit I may have gone a little overboard with this.

An absurd moment of clarity jolted me back to reality. It was a cold and dark evening, the night before Good Friday. Jan, Don and I were lined up on the deck in our PJs, ready to defend the house from this unseen enemy. Geoffrey had just driven up the driveway with our click-and-collect groceries. Don was wearing his head torch, and our outdoor table looked like it was prepared for surgery, only this surgical team was wearing pyjamas as we flicked on our latex gloves with hot soapy water, sanitiser and cloths at the ready. Time to wipe down all the groceries; no COVID germs were coming into *my* house.

As I looked around me at our family, all assembled on the deck in the dark, busy soaping our groceries before they were permitted through the front door, I realised that the world had gone mad. Or was it me? This wasn't normal; this wasn't how life was meant to be. And then I heard those dreaded words.

'Mum, where are the Easter eggs?' the kids cried.

A frantic search ensued but alas, the click-and-collect receipt confirmed our worst fears. The supermarket had run out of Easter eggs. The following day was Good Friday; the shops would be shut. We faced an eggless Easter.

Fast forward to the beginning of May 2022. A tingle of excitement washed over me as I called my sister's number. Geoffrey and I hadn't been anywhere in months, not since the start of the Omicron outbreak in New Zealand, but I was sick of hibernating like a hermit. Things were about to change.

'Guess what?' I prompted Helen, after saying hello.

'What have you done?' she replied suspiciously.

'I've booked a South Island holiday. We're coming down to see you for a week in Akaroa.'

'What? Really? When?'

'Next week,' I answered, giggling, because as usual I'd acted without thinking.

'Jeez, what did Geoffrey say?'

'Nothing, 'cos I haven't told him yet,' I replied, and we both laughed.

※

A week later Geoffrey and I drove off the ferry we'd taken from Wellington, beginning a road trip down the spectacular east coast of the South Island from Picton to Kaikōura. For miles the highway hugged the coastline beneath the snow-topped seaward Kaikōura Range which appears to rise straight from the rocky surf of the Pacific Ocean. Pulling into our accommodation for the night, I felt a sniffle coming on.

The next day we continued south, turning off at Greta Valley towards the coast and our planned lunch stop at Motunau. I straightened in my seat, craning my head as the landmarks of my childhood passed by: the cliffs where the UFO had appeared, our old bach where Dad nearly gassed us, the house where we'd partied with the boys, and Mum and Dad's former home.

Sitting at a picnic table, steaming coffee in hand, I stared out to sea towards the familiar, table-top shape of Motunau Island. The tide was out, leaving the river little more than a silvery trickle. A cool breeze ruffled my hair. Turning my head I looked towards the spot where the youth group's tent had been pitched, the playground where our children had laughed and played. The beach felt empty, lifeless; seagulls cried on the wind; pigeons swooped off the cliffs. *You can't go back; you can only go forwards*, I thought, blowing my nose. We packed up our things and headed on towards Akaroa in silence.

Rows of golden vines blanketed the rolling hill country of North Canterbury, leading towards Christchurch, city of my childhood. I was lost in thought with memories of Mum washing over me. She'd only been gone three months. *This time, Mum, I'm going to have a holiday without causing any trouble at all, just to prove it can be done.* Geoffrey skirted Christchurch and headed towards Banks Peninsula and our destination, the quaint seaside town of Akaroa. My nose dripped.

Sniffing and sneezing, I squirted three drops of carefully extracted and stirred snot solution onto the rapid antigen test (RAT) station and waited with bated breath. I felt well so assumed it was just my usual sinus symptoms starting up but I needed to check before seeing Helen the next day.

I looked up. Geoffrey was on the couch opposite me snoring, exhausted after carting all the groceries upstairs. Gazing around, I had a chance to survey the modern décor of the Akaroa holiday apartment while my snot sample did its thing. This was to be our home for the next week: kitchen and living room upstairs, two bedrooms and a bathroom downstairs, with a pretty garden patio leading off the back bedroom.

Directly in front of me, the door to the balcony was open, looking out over twinkling fairy lights decorating the shop across the street, beyond which the bush was alive with evening birdsong. The sound of raucous tūīs filled the air as the smell of fish 'n' chips wafted in, mingled with the scent of the sea. Seagulls circled, attracted by the lure of fresh fish. I glanced casually down at the RAT result.

'Oh bloody hell,' I yelled.

Geoffrey bolted upright, looking around startled.

'I've got COVID,' I wailed, staring in disbelief at the bright red line lit up in all its glory next to the T symbol, as if taunting me.

'What? You can't have,' gasped Geoffrey, fully awake now and leaping to his feet.

He glanced over my shoulder at the result sitting there on the big, wooden coffee table. There was absolutely no doubt. That was no faint sniff of a line; it was wide enough to be a flipping road marker. Geoffrey slumped back on the couch and we stared at each other, the full implication of this news sinking in.

No Lake Pukaki, no Aoraki Mount Cook, no Doubtful Sound cruise, thought Geoffrey.

How am I going to tell Helen?

'Well this is just bloody typical, isn't it? Somebody's having a laugh. Seriously, day flipping one and I've got bloody COVID. Me! Me, of all people! Even hermits have been out more than I have. I'm practically a germophobe recluse so how the heck did I get COVID?' I ranted in disbelief.

Blowing my nose loudly, I flopped back into the couch cushions, not knowing whether to laugh or cry. Geoffrey stared into space, still in shock. Muttering to myself and dabbing at my nose, I reached for my cell phone and called Helen's number. I heard her familiar voice answer, full of excitement.

'I've got COVID,' I blurted, my face grimacing, anticipating her disbelief and disappointment.

'It's lucky that I brought half the contents of our kitchen with us, isn't it?' I crowed smugly the next day.

Geoffrey rubbed his aching back and said nothing. Now that we were trapped for seven days, we at least wouldn't starve. I even had most of my specially prepared COVID kit with us. The wooden coffee table in front of me was now a receptacle for tissues, Vicks sniffers, Vicks VapoRub, thermometer, throat lozenges, oximeter, antihistamines, inhalers and Panadols. I was prepared. No bat disease was going to take me out!

'Damn!'

'What?' commented Geoffrey, sounding bored.

'All that homemade soup I prepared for COVID is at home in the freezer,' I grumbled.

I texted Helen and she dropped tinned chicken soup and a care package of local fudge on our doorstep before backing away. We waved at her from the balcony. Geoffrey ate the fudge. Oh well. I couldn't taste or smell anything anyway. I continued to sneeze, sniff and snivel in between ramming the Vicks sniffers firmly up each nostril.

'At least we've got the lovely patio area to enjoy,' I commented and headed downstairs to get some fresh air in the garden. When I opened the back door, I stopped and stared. What I'd thought the previous day was a garden sprinkler on a timer was still going. Copious amounts of water now spouted from our very own backyard geyser, pooling perfectly across our underwater patio. No wonder the bedroom felt damp and cold.

'Geoffrey,' I called, with a voice taking on a hint of hysteria. I heard his footsteps plodding slowly down the stairs. Appearing beside me he looked outside.

'Oh shit,' he uttered. 'Why can we never go away without drama?'

'Aaaaachooooo,' was my response. 'I'll go call the manager.' I sighed, slowly climbing the stairs while coughing up the odd bat particle.

Geoffrey followed me a few minutes later as I ended the call to the manager. He looked at me enquiringly.

'Is the plumber coming?' he asked.

'Nope,' I responded, 'he's got COVID.'

Geoffrey stared at me.

'Well are they sending another one?' he asked hopefully.

'Nope, small town, one plumber,' I added with a shrug.

To escape the constant sound of running water and smell of damp, we carted all our stuff into the front bedroom, containing two single beds. *Some holiday this is turning out to be*, I thought, blowing a fresh round of Omicron secretions into my hanky and coughing up half a lung. Geoffrey however was only too pleased to keep his distance from me.

Once it was established that I wasn't about to expire or turn into a bat (Geoffrey might disagree), we read the COVID isolation rules. We were allowed out for walks in the fresh air and could even walk right through the centre of the town if we so desired, with masks being advised but optional outdoors.

We decided to make the most of a bad situation and take advantage of the warm autumn weather to explore the plentiful scenic rural roads and bays. From the centre of Banks Peninsula's circular shape and emerald-green harbour, steep hillsides fan out like spidery veins towards the Pacific Ocean. Around the perimeter the ocean has cut deep, finger-like coves, home to little blue penguins, New Zealand fur seals and the endangered Hector's dolphin. Dry golden grass farms are interspersed with native bush, alive with bird song. Small, colourful settlements nestle around each bay, accessed by narrow, treacherous roads. Perfect for adventure drives with Geoffrey. After all, in our own car, how could we possibly infect anyone else?

On day three of adventure driving, we pulled in briefly at the waterfront away from the town as I wanted a photo of the lighthouse. No one was around but we stayed in the car. Geoffrey lowered his window to get a couple of shots for me as the lighthouse was on his side of the vehicle. He turned towards me to get my phone.

Suddenly from nowhere an unmasked lady stuck her entire head in Geoffrey's open window and said loudly, 'Jenny and Dave are coming.'

I looked around in alarm, wondering who the hell Jenny and Dave were. Geoffrey looked flummoxed. Without pausing long enough for me to shout, 'GET OUT OF OUR CAR. I'VE GOT COVID,' she carried right on.

'They're coming from Hamilton for the funeral. They arrive later at the airport. Sarah and Todd and all the kids too,' she warbled on. 'I'll pick them up on my way home. I live in Christchurch.'

'What funeral and who the hell are you?' I wanted to scream, but I was struck dumb, mouth hanging open, gaping at her aghast. I didn't know what to do. And before I could interject to try and tell her I had COVID, she continued.

'My grandmother's died. She's not having a normal casket though. She's having a woven willow one. I think that's OK.'

No offence, but I don't care what sort of casket she's having, I thought, and again, *Who the hell* are *you?*

'It's been hard on me, you know,' she shared.

Geoffrey nodded and murmured in sympathy. I subtly tilted my head away, rolled my eyes heavenward in sheer disbelief and took a deep breath. How was I going to tell her now? She was clearly cuckoo.

'I think we'll scatter her ashes. She didn't want to be buried. She had a thing about being underground,' she added.

Are we on Candid Camera? I wondered, scanning the scene.

'It will be a big funeral; everyone's coming,' she continued.

It'll be your *funeral if you're not careful, lady, going around shoving your head in people's cars. But how the hell do I tell her she's probably got COVID now?* I waited for a suitable interlude to impart this news.

Without pause she moved on, explaining to her captive audience of two how she'd brought her dog and what type of food it liked to eat. Mid-stream during the dog's dietary requirements spiel, I was finding it hard to focus. Having recoiled my head whilst trying to hold my breath, I think my oxygen levels were depleted. Geoffrey decided enough was enough and suddenly blurted, 'Gotta go. Bye.'

Revving the engine, he sped off as soon as the woman's head withdrew from our car. Phew. I exhaled noisily before sucking in a huge lungful of air and loudly blowing my nose. Geoffrey stared at me crossly.

'What?' I asked.

'You've clearly got some sort of wonky aura that draws in the nearest loon,' he grumbled.

'So much for proving I could have a holiday without causing any trouble.' I sighed quietly.

Geoffrey snorted loudly. 'Well you failed there. You've stuffed the whole holiday up royally, booked an apartment with a geyser in the backyard, attracted another nut job and possibly started a COVID superspreader event at the funeral of someone we don't even flaming know. It doesn't get much worse than that! You should come with a warning for anyone planning on travelling with Denise—don't do it!"

Now you've read my misadventures, perhaps some of you have drawn conclusions over who really is to blame for so many mishaps. Is it really Denise? Certainly on some of these occasions, I admit to attracting trouble. OK, *causing* it. But at times you have to wonder if the universe really is having a laugh at me. What with gypsies, a black cat, ghosts, aliens and quite a few oddballs making their way into my sphere, even *I* am beginning to think I attract them somehow. The jury is out.

Thank you for travelling alongside me, and if you've made it to the end, well done. Travelling tales may have been off the agenda for a while but this isn't the end of the Never a Dull Moment series. Book three is already scampering around in my head, just waiting to get out onto paper. I do hope you'll join our family for the next instalment.

This will be a comedy of rural capers, looking back at our move with two young children to a dilapidated old farmhouse in the country. Not knowing anything about rural life, I set out to fill our land with totally inappropriate animals. The results were a nightmare for poor Geoffrey and the neighbouring farmer. The house was found to be inhabited by more than just rats and possums. Throw in a territorial ghost and a visit by the Spiritualist church to try and oust it. Never a dull moment indeed.

MESSAGE FROM THE AUTHOR

I sincerely thank you for reading this book and I hope you enjoyed it. All authors greatly appreciate readers taking a few minutes to leave a review. It really makes a huge difference.

Amazon US: www.amazon.com
Amazon UK: www.amazon.co.uk
Amazon Australia: www.amazon.com.au
Goodreads: www.goodreads.com

I would be delighted if you followed me on Instagram: www.instagram.com/sharonhslm
If you click on the highlights tabs there, you'll be able to browse photos related to this book.

I'm happy to answer any questions you may have so do please get in touch with me by:
Email: sharon.hayhurst@xtra.co.nz
Facebook: www.facebook.com/sharon.hayhurst.3
Instagram: www.instagram.com/sharonhslm

If you enjoy reading memoirs, I recommend you pop over to the Facebook group We Love Memoirs to chat with me and other authors: www.facebook.com/groups/welovememoirs

AUTHOR PROFILE

Sharon writes comedy memoirs using her customary wicked sense of humour to share life's disasters and mishaps which seem to follow her around the globe. She is a pre-school teacher, author and trouble magnet who, when not causing trouble, lives on a rural property in New Zealand with her husband, Geoffrey, and an assortment of animals. Reading her books, you will feel as if you are along for the ride, sharing the back seat of the car with her kids as one calamity after another unfolds. Sharon writes as she travels, using her dry wit to share her sharply observed stories.

ACKNOWLEDGEMENTS

I would like to thank my family and my sister, Helen, for their continued support.

Enormous gratitude to Victoria Twead and Ant Press for their ongoing help and valuable advice. Jacky Donovan, you are the wonder woman of editing. Thank you.

A huge thank you to Joe Shepherd for so perfectly capturing the image I had in my mind and bringing it to life for the book's cover.

Printed in Great Britain
by Amazon